POWER OVER PANIC

Bronwyn Fox had panic disorder/agoraphobia for five years and for two of those years was housebound. She recovered using meditation and a mindfulness-based cognitive technique, and went on to develop an award-winning program for helping people with anxiety disorders. Bronwyn was a co-founder of the Panic Anxiety Disorder Association Inc (PADA) and has been counselling people with anxiety for more than fifteen years. This is the third edition of her bestselling book. For more information go to panicattacks.com.au.

POWER OVER PANIC

Overcoming panic and anxiety

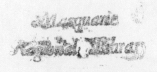

VIKING
an imprint of
PENGUIN BOOKS

VIKING

Published by the Penguin Group
Penguin Group (Australia)
250 Camberwell Road, Camberwell, Victoria 3124, Australia
(a division of Pearson Australia Group Pty Ltd)
Penguin Group (USA) Inc.
375 Hudson Street, New York, New York 10014, USA
Penguin Group (Canada)
90 Eglinton Avenue East, Suite 700, Toronto, Canada ON M4P 2Y3
(a division of Pearson Penguin Canada Inc.)
Penguin Books Ltd
80 Strand, London WC2R 0RL England
Penguin Ireland
25 St Stephen's Green, Dublin 2, Ireland
(a division of Penguin Books Ltd)
Penguin Books India Pvt Ltd
11 Community Centre, Panchsheel Park, New Delhi – 110 017, India
Penguin Group (NZ)
67 Apollo Drive, Rosedale, North Shore 0632, New Zealand
(a division of Pearson New Zealand Ltd)
Penguin Books (South Africa) (Pty) Ltd
24 Sturdee Avenue, Rosebank, Johannesburg 2196, South Africa

Penguin Books Ltd, Registered Offices: 80 Strand, London, WC2R 0RL, England

First published by Pearson Education Australia, 2001
This revised edition published by Penguin Group (Australia), 2010

10 9 8 7 6 5 4 3

Cover design by Elissa Christian © Penguin Group (Australia)
Text design by Karen Trump © Penguin Group (Australia)
Cover photograph by Brian Stablyk/Getty Images
Typeset in Berkeley Oldstyle 10/14.1pt by Post Pre-press Group, Brisbane, Queensland
Printed and bound in Australia by McPherson's Printing Group, Maryborough, Victoria

National Library of Australia
Cataloguing-in-Publication data:

Fox, Bronwyn.
Power over panic / Bronwyn Fox.
9780670074259 (pbk.)
Bibliography
Anxiety – Popular works
Panic attacks – Popular works
Panic disorders – Popular works
Stress management

616.85223

penguin.com.au

To Dr Eli Rafalowicz

'We paced along the lonely plain, as one who returns to his lost road,
and till he reaches it, seems to go in vain.'
Dante, 'Purgatorio' in *The Divine Comedy*

CONTENTS

Foreword **viii**
Introduction **1**

PART 1 **Understanding panic and anxiety**

1 What is happening to me? **15**

2 Panic attacks **19**

3 Anxiety disorders **24**

4 Secondary conditions **37**

5 Understanding our symptoms **50**

6 Therapies **69**

PART 2 **Prelude to recovery**

7 Simply not me **95**

8 Skilful compassionate action **105**

PART 3 **Managing panic attacks and anxiety**

9 Meditation **125**

10 Meditation – questions and answers **141**

11 Mind states **153**

12 Mindfulness as a cognitive technique **164**

PART 4 **Working through to recovery**

13 The layers of recovery **189**

14 The need to belong **213**

15 Unmasked **230**

PART 5 Recovery

16   The beginning   **245**

Appendix: Early intervention/prevention   **252**
Glossary   **266**
Further information   **267**
Bibliography   **268**
Acknowledgements   **271**
Index   **272**

Foreword

As far as I am concerned, Bronwyn Fox gave me back my life. I was struggling to overcome a very public nervous breakdown in 1994 when I received a request from Bronwyn to speak at an inaugural dinner for a fledgling anxiety disorders organisation. I get some pretty strange requests but I couldn't understand where this one had come from. Anxiety disorder? What the hell is an anxiety disorder, and why is this woman approaching me?

She had enclosed a copy of an earlier book of hers on anxiety and panic attacks. I had received a lot of pamphlets and advice from total strangers after my breakdown. They were mostly either Christian fundamentalist or New Age and went straight into the recycling bin. But this book was a revelation. This was me.

I recognised myself immediately. I can't tell you the relief I felt when I realised what was wrong with me. It had a name and it was treatable! Until then I had seen various therapists and not one of them had actually said to me, 'You have an anxiety disorder.' One therapist told me my problem of fear would be more manageable if I worked only with people I trusted. Great! My self-confidence is just about zero and this guy's encouraging me to become completely helpless. And this from a clinical psychologist.

Another psychologist tried waving a pen in front of my eyes. When that didn't work, she told me to wear a rubber band around my wrist and whenever I felt negative I was to snap the rubber band against my skin. While I was reacting to the pain, I was to replace the negative thought with a positive one. Well, my tolerance to pain must be greater than I imagined because it didn't have any effect, except for a slight tingling in my fingertips if I wore the rubber band for any length of time. How I was to manage any gangrene that developed, she didn't say.

When the fear started to paralyse me again, my shrink put me on a drug that had a rather unpleasant side effect: it made me disinhibited. Not a great quality for someone with social phobia. I would say or do the most inappropriate things at the most inappropriate times, and usually to people I really cared about. I was getting quite desperate. And it was costing me a fortune.

When we eventually met, I quizzed Bronwyn on where I could get help. She pointed me in the right direction. Eight sessions later I was back on my feet.

Cognitive therapy is deceptively simple; it's the commitment and repetition that makes it work. One day, the penny drops and you realise you now perceive things differently. You don't immediately jump to an irrational conclusion. I still use these skills to this day. Whenever I feel even the smallest amount of fear creeping up, I nip it in the bud.

In this book, Bronwyn explains very simply how to get your life back on track without drugs, just mind work and meditation. Meditation has a tremendous effect on the nervous system. I meditate twice daily, and any stress just evaporates after twenty minutes. This quiet time really allows you to appreciate yourself just as you are. It gives a stronger sense of self, and strong self-esteem is what good mental health is all about.

Bronwyn suffered from panic disorder for a number of years before devising this program. She is an inspiring teacher and a tireless crusader for the recognition of anxiety disorders, which are a major problem within the community. She has heaps and heaps of wisdom, which she shares with all. Make the most of this book. It will change your life.

Garry McDonald, actor

Introduction

It is extraordinary how one moment in time can change your whole life. The morning of my first panic attack was like any other morning. The only hint something was amiss was that I had not been feeling well for a few days. It wasn't enough to prevent me from working, although it was on my mind that morning as I drove to work. I had stopped at a red light and was waiting for it to turn green when the attack happened. One moment in time and my life, as I knew it, changed forever.

An electric shock surged through me, and my whole body reacted to the surge. And, to make things really interesting, I felt as if I had left my body. I could 'see' myself, and I could 'see' myself reacting. My heart was racing, I was having difficulty breathing, I felt dizzy and nauseous, and everything seemed unreal, including myself. I did what we all do. I panicked. And who wouldn't? All I wanted to do was get out of the car and run. Which wasn't a good idea, considering the five lanes of peak-hour traffic waiting at the red light and the other five lanes of traffic opposite me, still moving through the intersection on a green light.

Of course, I went to the doctor, and I went to the doctor, and I went to the doctor. I had more attacks and was extremely anxious about it happening again, and although I didn't know it at the time, guaranteed that it did.

I had no idea what was happening to me, and no matter how hard I fought it, I continued to get worse. Three months after my first panic attack, I learnt to meditate. Although I knew nothing about meditation, I felt it would be good for me. But at that point I was too confused and too frightened of what was happening to me to appreciate or understand the fundamental principles of meditation, and what it could do to help me.

I became suicidal as my life as I knew it was being destroyed, and it seemed that there was not a thing I could do to stop it. I was referred to a psychiatrist, who immediately diagnosed panic disorder. This in itself is extraordinary. I have met so many people who developed panic disorder in the early 1980s, and who weren't diagnosed until the late 1990s, and here I was, diagnosed within five months of it beginning.

The problem was I did not believe it. I knew I panicked, I knew I was anxious, but I kept thinking if only my psychiatrist would do something to stop the precipitating sensations, there would be no need for me to panic or be anxious. After all, I was a credit manager, and credit managers don't develop 'panic disorder'. 'This is not me, I'm not like this' became my constant refrain.

My doctor had prescribed tranquillisers within a few weeks of my first attack, but they did not stop the ongoing horror of my experience. When my psychiatrist changed the tranquillisers, the attacks kept on going. I could not understand why he couldn't just wave a magic wand and stop the sensations in their tracks. After all, he was a psychiatrist and isn't that what they are supposed to do?

As my disorder developed, I began to have difficulties doing all the normal things I had taken for granted. Getting to work, and actually staying at work, became a major problem. I would try to drive to work; sometimes I would make it, other times I couldn't and would leave my car on the side of the road or in the company car park and catch a taxi home. If I got to work, sometimes I could stay there but other times I would need to go home again. Sometimes after only five minutes! And these occasions became almost a daily event.

Within a year I had given up my job and was for all intents and purposes housebound. I could only travel to the local hospital to see my psychiatrist, or to go to the accident and emergency department when my attacks and anxiety became all too much. Thankfully, the hospital was only five minutes away.

Because I was 'not like this', I didn't tell my psychiatrist. He knew I had left work but he didn't know that I couldn't do any of the other normal things I used to do. I just kept hoping that it would all go away, that I would wake up one morning and, like the darkness of the night, it too would be gone. That didn't happen.

I knew when I commenced therapy that it was going to be for a limited time, as my psychiatrist was not going to be available in the new year. The therapy finished, and I stayed home except for the visits to accident and emergency or my doctor. Being housebound didn't mean an end to my attacks or my anxiety. They kept on keeping on. I lived and breathed them all day, and would be woken from sleep with an attack at night.

I began to meditate every day. Not because I thought it would help me – at that point I didn't think anything could – but rather, I used meditation as an escape from the nightmare I was living. What I didn't know was that mindfulness meditation is the oldest cognitive technique in the world. While I thought I was escaping, I was actually learning. Learning how to recover.

I would sometimes experience attacks during meditation, but I learnt not to care about them. They were exactly the same as the panic attacks I experienced during the day, and also at night, but within the quiet of meditation I learnt to let them happen. I didn't resist them as I normally would. Nor would I become caught up in my thoughts about them. The attacks would flash through me and be over within thirty seconds. Because I was not getting involved in my thoughts about the attacks, I felt no anxiety. I learnt that once they were over, I would move into the deeper stages of the all-encompassing quiet beauty of meditation. And that was all I wanted.

Gradually, I began to understand exactly what I was doing. I realised that I could learn to manage my daily attacks and anxiety in the same way that I did in meditation. I didn't need to spend my life sitting in a chair or on the floor meditating to get relief. Just as I had learnt to become aware of my thoughts during meditation, so I learnt to become aware of my thoughts during the day. By doing this, I saw for the first time how my thoughts were creating so much of my distress. I saw how my thoughts were actually turning on my anxiety and panic, and the more I saw this, the more I realised there was nothing to fear. I could see how my anxiety was being created moment to moment. And most importantly, I saw I had a choice in what I thought about.

I could *choose* not to think about anything that was going to keep my anxiety and panic going. I was aware of my thoughts, but I saw that I could either think about them and feel anxious, or I could simply let them go in the same way as I did in meditation. I was very aware that I needed to let the thoughts go, and not run from them or distract myself from them, as I had learnt that would only generate more anxiety. And so I began the process of being aware and letting go.

In the beginning, I would get caught up in my thoughts continually; my anxiety levels would rise, I would have an attack and I would panic. But as I worked to pull my thoughts back, time and again, I became involved in letting them go, rather than getting caught up in them.

Meditation had taught me how to let whatever happened during meditation to just simply happen. When I brought this technique into my everyday life, I learnt to let my attacks and my anxiety happen without resistance. As a result, my anxiety diminished and my attacks disappeared within thirty to sixty seconds, just as they had done in meditation. For me, this was amazing. Previously, my attacks could last for over sixty minutes at a time before I dropped back into a highly anxious state.

I began to drive again. I would make it to the bottom of the street before I would turn around and head home, driven by fear, anxiety and panic. I would get home, get control of my anxiety, and do it all over again. After that I was able to drive for half a kilometre before heading home in total panic. Then I was able to drive 1, 5, 10, 20 kilometres. My skills increased, and I learnt I could have an attack anywhere, at any time, and I could control it by letting go of my thoughts and by letting my anxiety just be there. 'So what!'

During this time I began to see recovery as a process, and I learnt to trust the process. I would make gains, only to be thrown back into panic and anxiety in the next hour or the next day. I learnt to understand why this was happening, and to work with it rather than against it. My recovery gained momentum and I began to experience days of freedom that I did not think were possible.

I was still taking tranquillisers, and decided that the time had come for me to go 'solo'. As I withdrew from my medication, my panic attacks and anxiety knew no bounds. No matter what I did, I could not regain control. Once again, I saw my life dissolve into fear, anxiety and panic. In those days, tranquillisers weren't thought to be addictive. My doctor told me that my symptoms were due to my disorder, and that no matter what I did, I would never recover from it. I had worked so hard to get my life back together again, and to be told it was all in vain was too much for me to bear.

I became suicidal again. Thankfully, my psychiatrist returned to work at the local hospital. He confirmed that my medication was addictive, and that my symptoms were those of drug withdrawal. I began a more structured withdrawal program under his and my doctor's supervision. I drew on the skills I had learnt through meditation, and was able to let the withdrawal symptoms happen and not become caught up in my thoughts about them. And slowly and surely I recovered.

The one question I had that I could not find an answer for was: why was I still having attacks? I was no longer frightened of my attacks, and I no longer panicked or felt anxious about them. At this stage of my recovery, I was very aware of my thoughts and there appeared to be no reason why these attacks, 'without the panic', were happening. But when I asked the question, all my doctor and psychiatrist could do was look at me in a slightly bemused way.

And so I continued to recover, still experiencing the odd attack without the panic, which really was odd! I returned to work as a credit manager, and I continued in therapy with my psychiatrist for a few more months.

At nights and on weekends I began to teach other people who had panic disorder, how to have an attack without the panic and how not to be anxious about the attacks. In those days, very few people were diagnosed as having panic disorder. At best, they were told they had agoraphobia, but the usual diagnosis was 'stress' or 'nerves'.

A few of us established an association for people with an anxiety disorder, and it grew very quickly. Together, we survived the ongoing lack of funds and resources, and the ever-growing number of people who needed our services. I continued to teach other people how to manage their attacks and anxiety by using meditation as a relaxation technique, and as a technique to learn to take control of thoughts and feeling states.

A couple of years after I had recovered, I attended a meditation festival in one of our city's parks. There were a number of meditation groups participating; most of them were handing out information and some were running 'how to meditate' sessions.

I walked over to the Tibetan Buddhist information booth, where an American monk was giving a talk on mindfulness, or insight meditation as it is also known. Much to my surprise, he described exactly the same technique that I had used to recover, and which I was teaching other people in my panic anxiety management programs. I was amazed, stunned and excited. Not only did the technique have a name, people had been practising it for the last 2500 years! Nowadays, mindfulness is recognised internationally as an effective cognitive technique and is being used in the prevention and treatment of stress, anxiety disorders, depression and chronic pain, amongst other conditions.

For me, it showed the universal nature of mindfulness, and how it can be used successfully irrespective of cultures and people's personal beliefs. A year later I moved into the local Buddhist Centre and studied with the Rinpoche, a Tibetan Lama, and his monks. I stayed there for two years.

In the early 1990s I was invited to speak at a conference about meditation in the United States. A different conference was being held a week later in the same vicinity, and as I was already going to be in the States, I registered to attend. One of the speakers, a recognised specialist in dissociation, was presenting a paper about dissociation and panic attacks. I wasn't really sure what dissociation was, but I thought it would be interesting.

The specialist spoke of dissociative states, including depersonalisation and derealisation, which are a feature of spontaneous panic attacks. Depersonalisation is the experience of feeling detached from the body, and derealisation is the experience that nothing seems real, including yourself.

Dissociation can also be described as a trance state, or altered state of consciousness. Many people who have spontaneous panic attacks have the ability to unknowingly self-induce these trance states. I saw very clearly that my attacks, without the panic, were the result of me unknowingly moving into a self-induced trance state. I couldn't believe it. I finally had my answer.

And so began a number of years of research. What we found was that many people who experience spontaneous panic attacks actually dissociate first and then panic as a result of the sensations and feelings of the trance state. We also found that the experience of the 'electric shock', burning heat and other sensations come as part of the trance state. Once we lost our fear of our dissociative states, we no longer panicked. All we were left with was the 'attack without the panic'! (Arthur-Jones & Fox, 1994.) Unfortunately, this link between dissociation and spontaneous panic attacks is rarely considered in current anxiety disorder treatment programs.

As the understanding of the disorders has developed over the years, there have been many major changes in their recognition and treatment. Many people are now being diagnosed either on first presentation to their doctor, or within a few weeks of their first panic attack. And more people now have access to effective treatment.

People often ask me my views in regards to medication. Medication can sometimes be necessary. I needed to take medication at one point. Medication can reduce the overall levels of distress and enable people to begin to learn the necessary cognitive skills that will enable them, ultimately, to manage their panic and anxiety by themselves in the long term.

I know from both personal and professional experience that working through to recovery can be difficult and confusing. This can be further complicated by the lack of trust and confidence people have in their own ability to recover.

When I talk about the recovery process, I use an analogy of climbing a steep cliff face. As a child, access to our local beach was via a pathway constructed down such a cliff face. The return journey home meant negotiating the pathway back to the top of the cliff.

Standing at the bottom of the cliff, the pathway leading back to the top was a steep, straight climb that came to an end about halfway to the top. There was a seat carved out of stone at this point, as an acknowledgement of how hard the climb could be. From there, the pathway cut across the cliff face for a number of metres. It then turned back and cut across the cliff face in the other direction, before turning yet again to cross the cliff face in the other direction. And so it continued in this way until reaching the top.

At the bottom of the cliff, the view was limited to the immediate surroundings. As you walked up the pathway, the view began to open up and expand. More of the coastline came into view. At the top, the view seemed limitless. The sea, the sky and the coast-line appeared to stretch into infinity.

Before our disorder developed, and during our experience of an anxiety disorder, we have a limited view of ourselves and our environment. As we begin the recovery process, it can seem like a steep, hard climb. We can have a sense of not knowing where we are and where the path will lead us. The more we continue to work with the recovery process, the more our perception of ourselves and our disorder expands. We begin to understand and trust the process as we appear to move in one direction, only to turn in another. We become familiar with the rest stops and signposts along the way. We recover, and we are free and remain free. Our view of ourselves and our panic and anxiety has opened and expanded. Our perception has changed. We see the 'bigger picture'.

Recovery is much like peeling an onion. It can sometimes sting and it can make us cry. Mindfulness teaches us how to work with our obvious, 'loud' panic- and anxiety-inducing thoughts, and it teaches us how to control them. As our mindfulness skills develop, we begin to see the more subtle, albeit conscious, layers of thoughts that drive so much of our anxiety and depression. These thoughts all revolve around 'who we think we should be', and our need for constant approval from everyone else.

Being 'who we think we should be' means that any sense of self and identity is dependent on what other people think of us. It is not centred within ourselves. As we see these more subtle layers of thought, we also see that our anxiety can become our teacher. It can teach us about ourselves, and it can show us how to become who we could be. If we heed its message, we can find the answer to the question, 'Who am I?' And our sense of self and identity shifts and becomes centred within us.

The issues relating to a healthy sense of self and self-esteem are overlooked in most anxiety disorder treatment strategies; sometimes they are discounted altogether. The various theories see anxiety disorders as being due to a chemical imbalance or learned behaviour. One therapy targets one aspect, a different therapy targets another. Even when combined together, they do not provide a holistic approach that also addresses the lack of a sense of self and related self-esteem issues.

While treatments can medicate or CBT the disorders away, or partially away, people are still at risk of further episodes of their disorder because the inner conflict remains. And that inner conflict is the question 'Who am I and who should I be?' versus 'This is me and all I could be.'

All of us who have recovered now realise the significance and profundity of the recovery process. Despite the destruction of our lives through our disorder, everything that was taken away from us during that time has been given back to us in ways we never dreamed of: the freedom and the joy to be who we are. And there is no greater gift than this.

And for me, it was all because of one moment in time.

Bronwyn Fox
2009

Part 1

Understanding panic and anxiety

CHAPTER 1

What is happening to me?

PANIC ATTACKS

Imagine you are relaxing in front of the television, having dinner with friends, at a cinema or theatre, driving to work, reading a book or in bed asleep. Without warning, you feel an electric shock or burning heat move through your body. Your heart begins to race. You have difficulty breathing, and you experience pain in your chest and left arm. You feel dizzy and nauseous, and everything seems unreal, as if you are looking through a white or grey mist. You may even feel as if you have become separated from your body, and are actually looking at yourself. Your body begins to shake and tremble, and thoughts race through your mind: 'What's happening to me?' You feel as if you want to run, as fast as you can, to get away from whatever it is you are experiencing. And most of us 'run' to our doctor or to the accident and emergency department of our local hospital.

What if?

'You're having a panic attack,' says the doctor.

'Yes, of course I'm panicking. Wouldn't you?' you ask somewhat incredulously. 'But tell me what's happening to me! I'm having a heart attack, aren't I? A stroke? Is it a brain tumour, a seizure? It's all right, you can tell me. Please tell me.'

'You are having a panic attack,' repeats the doctor.

A panic attack? How can that be? The experience seems so much more than a 'panic attack'. 'Are you sure?' you ask.

What if the doctor has made a mistake, overlooked something, mixed up the results of the clinical tests? What if it happens again? What if this was some sort of warning? What if it's worse next time?

With each thought, our fear and our anxiety increase. Try as we might, we simply can't stop thinking about it. The attack happens again. The doctor tells us the same thing. Our thoughts race, our fears increase and the cycle of fear, anxiety and panic begins.

CASE HISTORIES

Laura

It had been a long and difficult week, and Laura was glad she now had some time to herself. She curled up on the sofa with a book she had been wanting to read. As she relaxed, she felt the tension ease from her body and found herself drifting to sleep.

Without warning, Laura felt a wave of incredible energy surge through her body. As it moved through her, her heart rate doubled and she had difficulty breathing. She felt light-headed and dizzy as a wave of nausea swept over her, and she began to perspire.

Laura jumped up and ran outside to her husband. 'Help me, something is happening to me,' she said. 'I don't know what, but something is very wrong.'

Terri

Terri closed the door to the children's room and walked into the lounge. It had been a long day and she was looking forward to being able to relax. Suddenly a tingling feeling went through her body, and it felt like her heart missed a couple of beats. It was as if a volume control had been turned up in her head, as the sound of the television and the cars in the street seemed intolerably loud. The floor felt like it was moving up and down, and Terri began to experience pins and needles in her arms and feet. She was frightened by what was happening to her. She was alone with the children and her husband was not due home for an hour. Terri's fear intensified.

Although there is now far greater awareness of anxiety disorders within the community, and within the health professions, we still don't understand what is happening to us. Other than the feelings of panic, the words 'panic attack' do not bear any resemblance to what we are experiencing.

The explanations we are given about our attacks do not make sense to us. We are told we have a chemical imbalance, or that we are suffering from an overactive 'fight and flight' response, but these explanations do not adequately explain our experience. And they leave us with enormous doubt and fear that the doctor has made a mistake.

We are terrified by what is happening to us. We panic about our attacks, we panic about our panic, and we become anxious about our anxiety. Our thoughts race this way, that way and every way in between. And we are drawn back time and again into the fear and our expanding cycle of distress. We can go back and forth to our doctor, to accident and emergency departments, we can seek a second and third, perhaps even a tenth opinion, and all we hear are the words 'panic attack' and 'anxiety'.

We become embarrassed and ashamed by seeking reassurance from our doctor, because we know there is no one who recognises the magnitude of our experience. As so many of us say: 'Stop this from happening to me and there will be no reason for me to panic or be anxious.'

While it is normal to be extremely frightened and confused by what is happening to us, we need to break through this cycle of fear. We need to acquire the knowledge and understanding about panic attacks, anxiety and anxiety disorders, and we need to learn how to manage them. Knowledge and understanding give us the power to do so.

CHAPTER 2

Panic attacks

In 1994 the American Psychiatric Association (APA) identified three different types of panic attacks: spontaneous, specific and situationally predisposed (APA, 1994). Until that time, no specific distinction was made between the characteristics of panic attacks. A panic attack was a panic attack – a phobic response to situations and/or places. People with panic disorder were thought to have a fear of 'open spaces' or a fear of 'the market place'. That they were not frightened of open spaces or the market place was never considered. No wonder so many people didn't recover!

The American Psychiatric Association describes a panic attack as 'a discrete period of intense fear or discomfort that is accompanied by at least four of thirteen physical or cognitive symptoms'. The experience of less than four symptoms is known as a 'limited symptom attack' (APA, 1994). These symptoms include:
- Palpitations, pounding heart or accelerated heart rate
- Sweating
- Trembling or shaking
- Sensations of shortness of breath or smothering

- Feeling of choking
- Chest pain or discomfort
- Nausea or abdominal distress
- Feeling dizzy, unsteady, light-headed or faint
- Derealisation: feelings of unreality
- Depersonalisation: feeling detached from oneself
- Fear of losing control or going crazy
- Fear of dying
- Numbness or tingling sensations
- Chills or hot flushes

The symptoms of panic attacks and anxiety can be quite varied, with any number of symptoms being experienced at the same time. I will discuss these symptoms in detail in Chapter 5.

TYPES OF PANIC ATTACKS

While panic attacks are associated with a number of anxiety disorders, not everyone who experiences a panic attack develops a disorder. Some people may experience one panic attack and never have another. Other people may experience an occasional panic attack, but they don't become caught up in the ongoing cycle of fear that so many of us become trapped in.

The three different types of panic attacks identified by the American Psychiatric Association define the relationship between these attacks and the individual anxiety disorders.

Spontaneous (uncued) panic attacks

This type of panic attack appears to come 'out of the blue', without warning, and it is this type of panic attack that is associated with panic disorder. Spontaneous panic attacks are not related to any specific situation or place. They can simply happen, regardless of what we are doing at the time.

Specific (cued) panic attacks

People who have social phobia, obsessive compulsive disorder or post-traumatic stress disorder experience these types of attacks. The attacks are specific to the various fears related to the individual disorder (see Chapter 3). People with panic disorder don't usually experience these types of attacks.

Situationally predisposed panic attacks

People with panic disorder may experience this type of attack. Some people with panic disorder can be predisposed to panic attacks in certain situations or places, although they are not frightened of the particular situation or place itself. For example, they may experience panic attacks while driving or while asleep. Sometimes they will have them; at other times they won't. They are predisposed to attacks in these situations, but the attacks themselves are not in response to any particular fear of driving or of sleep.

People with one of the other anxiety disorders can also experience this type of attack. For example, someone with social phobia may experience a situationally predisposed panic attack while speaking with someone, but at other times they may not. However, their panic attack is specific to their fear of embarrassing themselves in some way (see Chapter 3).

CASE HISTORIES

Alex

Alex disliked staff meetings and social functions, and he did whatever he could to avoid them. He felt more comfortable just doing his job and avoiding personal interaction with other staff. Now the new owners of the business had arranged a dinner for all members of staff and their partners and, like it or not, he thought he had to attend.

Alex had been feeling uncomfortable all day, and he knew his anxiety levels were very high. As he and his wife sat down at their table, the people next to them began to make conversation. He began to panic. His heart began to race, his breathing became short and shallow, his face was flushed as he began to perspire heavily, and his hands trembled violently. As he tried to control his anxiety, he thought to himself, 'What are they going to think? I knew I shouldn't have come.'

Jessica

Jessica turned on the ignition of her car. She was feeling very anxious. 'Is it going to happen today?' As she pulled out of her driveway, she tried to rationalise with herself for the hundredth time.

Jessica wasn't frightened of driving; in fact, she used to enjoy driving before she began to experience spontaneous panic attacks. But there was one set of traffic lights where she would sometimes have an attack. There was no pattern to it. Sometimes she would have an attack while waiting at the traffic lights, or it would happen after she had driven through the intersection; on other days there were no attacks at all.

Someone told her she was frightened of that particular inter-section, but she said that was ridiculous. She was frightened of the attacks and their unpredictable nature; it had nothing to do with the intersection.

Isabel

The end of Isabel's shift was in sight. Another hour and she could go home, but first she had to hand over to the nurses on afternoon shift. She felt her stomach tighten and her anxiety increase. Isabel had never had problems talking in front of people before, but the thought of today's handover terrified her. She remembered the last weeks and how it had become increasingly difficult for her to appear 'normal'.

Isabel's first panic attack had happened at work. Although she knew what was wrong with her, she was having enormous difficulty trying to 'pull herself together'. No matter how hard she tried, she couldn't control what was happening to her. She didn't think the other nurses would understand if they found out, and she was too frightened to ask any of the doctors about it because she was afraid they would make her leave her job at the hospital.

CHAPTER 3

Anxiety disorders

STATISTICS

Although symptoms of panic disorder were first noted in the 1800s (Boyd et al, 1991), anxiety disorders weren't recognised by the American Psychiatric Association as a discrete group of disorders until 1980. Anxiety disorders include panic disorder, social phobia, post-traumatic stress disorder, obsessive compulsive disorder and generalised anxiety disorder.

Many people are surprised when they learn that 14 per cent of the adult population experience an anxiety disorder (ABS, 2009), and that anxiety disorders represent the most common mental health problem in the community. While there is now much more awareness of panic attacks and anxiety, anxiety disorders are still hidden within the community. When we begin to develop an anxiety disorder, we feel as if we are the only person in the world experiencing this level of distress. We are not being narcissistic; it is more that we can't believe other people would be feeling this degree of distress without the disorders being more widely acknowledged in the community.

Anxiety disorders affect people right across the socioeconomic spectrum and across all age groups. While many people will develop an anxiety disorder between their late teens and mid-thirties, children can also develop a disorder and so can people in their forties, right through to their eighties.

People often ask me if the increase in the number of people with an anxiety disorder is due to the escalating pressures and demands of life. While this can be a factor, the main reason for the increase is because in the recent past many people were simply not being diagnosed at all, and they lived their life suffering from stress or 'nerves'.

UNDERSTANDING

Part of the overall problem in understanding the severity of anxiety disorders lies in the words 'anxiety' and 'panic attack'. There is a marked difference between the 'normal' experience of anxiety and the anxiety that becomes so extreme that people become disabled by it.

Everyone will have experienced anxiety at some time in their life. Some people have difficulty accepting that the experience of an anxiety disorder is different from their own individual experience of anxiety. Their anxiety may not have affected them to any great extent; it passed of its own accord and was no longer a problem. As a result, they find it difficult to accept that a person with an anxiety disorder experiences something different from normal anxiety. It is from this perspective that some people label others with an anxiety disorder as 'weak' and tell them to 'pull themselves together'.

The same applies to the words 'panic attack'. Often when I am talking publicly about panic attacks, someone will make the comment: 'I know what it is like. I had a panic attack the other

day. I was running late for work and could not find my car keys.'
While the person may have panicked about finding their keys, the
experience of a panic attack is not that simple or straightforward.

People with panic disorder, and sometimes people with one of
the other anxiety disorders, do not recognise that their symptoms
are anxiety and panic attacks, especially if they have a dissociative
component to their attacks.

CAUSES

Except in the case of post-traumatic stress disorder, the causes of
anxiety disorders are still not known. Research suggests there is a
'genetic contribution' to the development of panic disorder (APA,
1994). It is not unusual for us to discover that other family members may have had, or still have, the disorder. In our parents' and
grandparents' generation, people were never diagnosed and coped
with it as best they could. In previous generations, the disorder
may have been 'hiding' behind an alcohol dependency or behind
what we consider to be 'eccentric' behaviour in a family member.

The genetic aspect always raises questions: 'What about my
children? Will they start to have panic attacks?' If they do, early
intervention strategies will be able to minimise or prevent the
development of an anxiety disorder. Hopefully, the necessary
resources for this will be more readily available in the future. Also,
as we recover, we will be in an ideal position to assist our children in a number of ways. Firstly, helping them understand their
anxiety or panic attacks and how to manage them; and secondly,
ensuring that the child is given an appropriate referral to a psychologist who specialises in childhood anxiety.

Panic attacks and anxiety can be triggered by any number of
experiences – a major life stress, physical illness, menopause,

influenza or another virus, the birth of a child, studying for exams, experimentation with marijuana or other similar drugs.

On occasion, there may be a time lag of up to twelve months between a major life stress and the initial panic attack. The effects of the major life stress can be compounded by ongoing day-to-day stress, which ultimately triggers our first panic attack or our anxiety. Yet it is not so much the stress itself that creates our anxiety as the way we perceive and deal with the stress.

Sometimes there doesn't appear to be any reason at all for the development of anxiety or panic attacks. This only adds to our confusion. We usually fail to recognise the various stresses in our lives, or simply write them off as not being factors. It can help to make a list of past and current events in our lives. When we see these events written down, the reason for the panic attacks and anxiety becomes obvious.

Much of the research into the causes of anxiety disorders has centred on panic disorder, and various theories have been suggested.

The biological model presupposes a chemical imbalance, but it is not known if the chemical imbalance is either the cause or the effect of the attack (APA, 1994). If this was known, everyone would be able to use a specific medication and get on with their lives. As it is, some people can use most types of medication without experiencing any difficulties; other people may only be able to use a certain few medications, while a number of other people are unable to use any medication at all.

Psychodynamic theory looks at causes related to childhood (APA, 1994). While this can be so, people also need other management strategies in order to deal with their panic anxiety in their day-to-day lives. As people have said to me, 'How is working on my past going to get me out of the house today?' Once people have the necessary management skills, working on past issues can become the prevention 'strategy' of a future in which there is little possibility of a return of the disorder. I discuss this further in Chapter 15.

Behaviour theories suggest that anxiety disorders are learnt behaviours, and recovery means unlearning these previous limiting behaviours (APA, 1994). This also includes how to 'unlearn' our panic- and anxiety-producing thoughts.

Another theory is the role dissociation plays in panic disorder and post-traumatic stress disorder. Putman (1989) suggests that 'dissociative phenomena exist on a continuum' and range from a 'normal process to the most severe'.

Over the years, I have found that the ability to dissociate – that is, to enter a trance state, an alteration of consciousness – is very common in people who experience spontaneous panic attacks. Two dissociative symptoms, depersonalisation and derealisation, are listed amongst the most common symptoms in spontaneous panic attacks (APA, 1994). Research also suggests that nocturnal panic attacks occur 'during the transition from stage two to stage three sleep' (Uhde, 1994) – in other words, during an alteration of consciousness.

It is interesting to note that once people who dissociate have an understanding of the phenomena, they report the experience of dissociation as being the trigger for some of their panic attacks. I will discuss dissociation in more detail in Chapter 5.

The recovery process can incorporate all these theories. Some people may need to use medication while they develop their mindfulness or other cognitive skills. Once these skills are mastered, they may then choose to work on any current or past personal issues that are contributing to the anxiety and depression. Ultimately, it is a personal choice as to the treatment strategies people wish to use.

CASE HISTORY

Tom

It was 1 a.m. Tom had been asleep since 11 p.m. He was due to return to his teaching position the next day, after two weeks' school holidays. Tom woke with a start as his body jerked violently and a surge of heat went through him. His heart was pounding and he was gasping for breath. His shoulders and arms began to ache, and he felt as if he was going to faint. Tom woke his wife, who then called an ambulance as they both feared he was having a heart attack.

PANIC DISORDER

Panic disorder is the fear of having a spontaneous panic attack (APA, 1994) – *fear* being the operative word. It is the fear of having a spontaneous panic attack that is the driving force in the development of panic disorder.

Panic disorder is diagnosed after a person has experienced 'at least two' spontaneous panic attacks followed by one month or more of 'persistent concern' about having another attack (APA, 1994). It is this 'persistent concern', or fear, that not only causes much of our distress, but also makes us more vulnerable to having another attack. And many of us do. It is not unusual for people to begin to have one or more panic attacks a day, and to experience pervasive anxiety in anticipation of having another.

For so many of us, recovery has been the loss of the fear of having one of these attacks. Once we lose our fear, we 'lose' our disorder and our ongoing anxiety about having another attack.

Because of the intensity of the attack, most people feel as if they are:

- Having a heart attack
- Going to die
- Going insane
- Losing control in some way
- Having a stroke
- Suffering from a brain tumour

Part of our fear includes a number of secondary fears in association with the major fears listed above. These secondary fears include the fear that:

- the doctor has overlooked something in the original assessment
- the diagnosis is incorrect
- the clinical test results have been mixed up with another person's
- the 'big' attack with its major fears will occur
- we will not be able to access medical attention if the 'big' attack or other attacks occur
- we will be alone when the 'big' attack or other attacks occur
- we will have an attack in front of people

SOCIAL PHOBIA

People with social phobia fear they will embarrass themselves, or make a fool of themselves, and will be judged by others in a negative way, in social or 'performance' situations (APA, 1994). Some people with social phobia may also have a fear of blushing. While many of us can feel anxious in these situations, social phobia is diagnosed when the fear significantly disrupts normal day-to-day living.

These fears can occur in any number of situations, including:

- Initiating or maintaining conversations
- Carrying out everyday activities such as shopping or walking down the street
- Eating or drinking in front of others
- Public speaking, either professionally or socially
- In an office situation, for example, writing out receipts, using the photocopier while other people are waiting to use the machine
- Writing or signing documents in front of people, such as filling out bank forms or signing credit card receipts
- Using an ATM machine
- Being in a crowd

People may experience a panic attack in any of these situations, and the attack is specific to the fear of embarrassing or making a fool of themselves.

OBSESSIVE COMPULSIVE DISORDER

Obsessive compulsive disorder (OCD) means being obsessed by 'persistent ideas, thoughts, impulses or images that cause marked anxiety or distress' (APA, 1994). People can be made extremely anxious by one or more of these obsessions, and their life becomes severely disrupted as a result. While they recognise that their compulsions are excessive and unreasonable, they are unable to control them, no matter how hard they try.

Although such obsessions are not based on 'real life' concerns, the anxiety and panic that results can be severe. A compulsion is a reaction to an obsession, and is used as a way of trying to stop the anxiety or the feared event. For example:

- Obsession: the fear of becoming contaminated by germs – this can lead to compulsive hand washing and cleaning
- Obsession: repeated doubts that electrical appliances have not been switched off – this can lead to compulsive checking and rechecking
- Obsession: a need to compulsively hoard everything and anything in case it is needed in the future

Other compulsions that can be used in an effort to stop or prevent obsessive thoughts include praying, counting or continually repeating certain words.

POST-TRAUMATIC STRESS DISORDER

Post-traumatic stress disorder (PTSD) can develop following an event or events in which the person 'experienced, witnessed or was confronted with' a situation that was life threatening to themselves or other people (APA, 1994). These can include:
- A major car accident or other serious trauma
- Being a victim of physical or sexual assault or rape
- Being a victim of an armed robbery
- Experiences of war
- Experiencing a natural disaster such as bushfires, cyclones, hurricanes or earthquakes
- Having a life-threatening illness

People who have experienced these events may have ongoing persistent thoughts about them. They may have flashbacks in which they believe they are actually living through the event again, or nightmares in which they relive the experience. Many people will have a specific panic attack in situations or places similar to, or reminiscent of, the event.

As an example, people who have experienced the devastation of bushfire may have a panic attack on days when the fire danger is high, or if they hear fire sirens. This panic attack is specific to the trauma they experienced during a bushfire.

Panic disorder can be secondary to post-traumatic stress disorder. On occasions, people will seek treatment for their panic disorder but will be too frightened or ashamed to speak of the traumatic event or events that preceded it. This is especially so in matters relating to childhood abuse. An English study found that 63.6 per cent of young women with panic disorder who were interviewed came from 'difficult childhood backgrounds', which included 'parental indifference, sexual and physical abuse' (Brown & Harris, 1993).

In addition to the flashbacks and nightmares, people with PTSD may also experience (APA, 1994):

- Difficulty falling asleep or sleeping
- Irritability or outbursts of anger
- Difficulty concentrating
- Hyper vigilance
- Exaggerated startle response

GENERALISED ANXIETY DISORDER

Generalised anxiety disorder is diagnosed when a person experiences excessive 'anxiety and worry' about particular real-life events that may or may not happen, for a period of at least six months (APA, 1994). These events can include fears and worries about their children, partner, family members or close friends, financial concerns, a work situation or a specific planned event.

People with generalised anxiety disorder will often comment to me that they have been worriers for most of their life. This worry can become all-pervasive and is accompanied by ongoing anxiety symptoms.

COMBINATIONS

It is not unusual for people to have fears and symptoms from all of the above disorders. People with panic disorder usually have ongoing anxiety. They may also have aspects of obsessive compulsive disorder, social anxiety and, in some instances, post-traumatic stress disorder.

CASE HISTORIES

Sam

Sam drove his truck out of the depot and onto the road that would take him to the freeway. He wiped the perspiration from his forehead. His hands were trembling. He had to keep going; this time – he needed to make his deliveries. He couldn't go back to the depot and say he was sick. Once more, and he knew he would lose his job. His stomach was churning, and the further away he was from the depot, the worse his anxiety and panic became. All Sam wanted to do was to go home. He didn't know how much more he could take. Over the last twelve months he had stopped doing most of the things he used to enjoy – playing or watching sport, having a few drinks with friends, going for a drive with his family. Now he just stayed home. It took all his energy just to get to work and get through the day.

Julia

'I get really confused about which anxiety disorder I have,' said Julia. 'I do have spontaneous panic attacks; I get that "not seeming real" feeling, like I am spaced-out. I am anxious most of the time about having another panic attack, but I also have other fears and other obsessional thoughts.' Julia hesitated, took a deep breath and continued. 'I am also frightened that I am going to catch some disease and pass it on to my family. It is so difficult to do anything. It is a nightmare going shopping or being around a lot of people. I carry an antibacterial gel, but I still spend most of my time washing my hands with soap and water. They are almost red raw.' She held her hands up to show her counsellor.

'It is okay, Julia. Thank you for telling me,' replied her counsellor. 'It is important that I know everything you are experiencing. This way I can help you more effectively. These thoughts are in the obsessive compulsive disorder category. A number of people with panic disorder also have these thoughts. And although it is very distressing, you can learn to manage them in the same way as your other anxiety and panic thoughts.'

Colin

Colin had always been shy at school. He had a couple of close friends who didn't make a fuss or tease him if he blushed on occasion, or if his voice trembled sometimes. They all played cricket for the local team. Colin loved the game and gave his all during each summer. So much so, he was made captain of the team.

Colin started to feel anxious most of the time and he began

to have trouble sleeping at night. He was excited at being chosen as captain, but he was also worried. He was frightened that he would be found out, that he was not as good a player as he was thought to be. He was also frightened that he was going to embarrass himself in some way, or make a fool of himself. Every time he addressed the team, his voice trembled, his face flushed and his hands shook. He believed that as captain he had a certain image to uphold, and he felt that he was falling short of who he was expected to be. He wasn't sure what to do. Try as he did, he could not 'pull himself together', and he lived in a state of constant anxiety.

Colin counted down the weeks to the end of the season and was pleased when it ended. Despite his difficulties, the team won all their games and was the top team in the district. He also won the district's best-player award.

Everyone assumed that Colin would be captain again next summer, but he wasn't sure if he could go through all the anxiety again. Despite his achievements, he still felt he was a fraud and worried that he would make a fool of himself at some point.

Earlier in the season a friend had suggested he see a psychologist. Colin wasn't sure if it would have made a difference to how he felt, but now he decided to go to see one. Perhaps a psychologist could prevent his anxiety or at least get it to manageable levels before next summer.

CHAPTER 4

Secondary conditions

In the past, and even now, the lack of understanding and effective treatment play a significant role in the development of anxiety disorders and the secondary conditions associated with them. Many people go on to develop agoraphobia and major depression as a result of their disorder. They can also develop an addiction to or dependency on prescribed medication, while others can develop an alcohol dependency.

Most people with an anxiety disorder will say, 'If only I had known what was happening to me; if only I was taught how to manage my anxiety and panic, none of this [the secondary conditions] would have happened.' It is astounding that early-intervention strategies for people with anxiety disorder are not seen as a priority within the health system. Early-intervention strategies can minimise or prevent the development of anxiety disorders and can prevent the development of the secondary conditions. This can reduce the individual's considerable suffering and reduce the enormous healthcare costs associated with the disorders (see Appendix).

Without adequate understanding and treatment, we do not effectively control what is happening to us, so we begin to develop other forms of control in an effort to ease our situation. Ironically and tragically, many of the controls we use become secondary conditions, helping to compound and perpetuate our disorder.

AGORAPHOBIA – AVOIDANCE BEHAVIOUR

Agoraphobia is one such control, and for many people it has meant a lifetime of limitation. Until panic disorder was recognised in 1980, agoraphobia was considered to be the primary problem. It was defined as a fear of open spaces or the market place, and older-style behavioural programs focused on this fear. But people were not frightened by open spaces or the market place; they were frightened of having a panic attack in any space or place. It didn't matter where they were or what they were doing, the fear of having a panic attack was always with them.

Agoraphobia in panic disorder is now recognised as 'anxiety about being in situations or places from which help may not be available in the event of having an uncued or situationally predisposed attack'. The situation 'is endured with marked distress or anxiety . . . or may require the presence of a companion' (APA, 1994).

Agoraphobia in social phobia is avoidance behaviour relating to social situations. In obsessive compulsive disorder it is avoidance behaviour relating to the particular obsessive thoughts. In post-traumatic stress disorder it is avoidance of stimuli related to the trauma (APA, 1994). Although the avoidance behaviour is limited to the specifics of the individual disorder, it can be all-encompassing.

Some people become housebound, totally avoiding certain

situations or places after their first panic attack. In other cases, the avoidance behaviour may be gradual, becoming increasingly restricting, or it may be permanently limited to one or two situations or places. People may have occasional panic attacks for years before avoidance behaviour sets in. In this case, the onset of avoidance behaviour is not a result of the panic attack itself but is usually a fear of a new symptom of anxiety.

Agoraphobia can affect people in different degrees. It can also affect the same person in different degrees at different times. It is a multifaceted and multi-contradictory condition. Learning to work with our avoidance behaviour is of course a major part of the recovery process, and I discuss this in detail in Chapter 13.

CASE HISTORIES

Jan

The wedding of Jan's daughter was six months away and the planning was gaining momentum. Instead of feeling excited, Jan was feeling desperate. What if she had a panic attack on the day of the wedding? What if she had to leave the church or the reception? What would everyone think? She didn't want to make a fool of herself or disrupt the wedding in any way. What if she couldn't even make it to the wedding at all? She was feeling anxious about it already, yet it was still six months away. Jan wanted to prevent her anxiety from increasing, but she didn't know how.

Marilyn

Marilyn's counsellor had told her that clinging to the memory of her first panic attack was not helping her as she worked on her recovery. Marilyn became quite angry with the counsellor. What did the counsellor know, anyway? That first panic attack was dreadful.

Marilyn had been in the local shopping mall when it happened. She had no idea what it was and had thought she was dying. She had asked people to help her but they hadn't responded. They must have thought she was either drunk or crazy. Marilyn had to get back to her car and drive herself home, where she stayed for the next four years.

Every time Marilyn tried to go out, she would think of her first attack and naturally she would become anxious. She didn't want to go through that again. How could she not think about that attack? It was the attack that had caused all the ongoing problems. Marilyn thought the counsellor, like all the rest she had seen, didn't really understand and wouldn't be able to help her.

AVOIDANCE BEHAVIOUR

I have always seen our avoidance behaviour in three different ways.

Avoidance as an overall defence

In the first instance our avoidance behaviour is an overall defence against further panic attacks and anxiety. Such avoidance, either partial or total, does not necessarily mean a cessation of these, but for many of us it can mean relative safety and, most importantly, privacy.

We can become restricted in where we can and can't go. We

may find we can travel within a certain radius of a few kilometres of home, and do everything we normally do in relative safety and comfort. Once outside this invisible boundary, our anxiety soars. As an overall control of the disorder, we stay within certain boundaries. This may mean becoming restricted not only to the house, but to one room. But even then the anxiety and panic attacks can remain.

Our avoidance behaviour can also be very subtle and gradual, as our area of relative 'safety' diminishes over time. We are able to do some things one day, only to find ourselves unable to do them the next. The cost of this defence can be high, as it can mean a total breakdown of our previous lifestyle.

Anticipatory anxiety

The second category of avoidance behaviour is caused by anticipatory anxiety, the 'what ifs?'. This category differs from the first in its defence and control. Avoidance as a defence is an overall, ongoing attempt to control further panic attacks and anxiety; anticipatory anxiety is a defence against a specific spiral of high anxiety.

Anticipatory anxiety is the fear of having a panic attack or being anxious while meeting a specific commitment. The overall defence against ongoing anxiety and panic attacks sometimes reduces them to a manageable level. However, the relative safety is lost when we have to break through our invisible boundaries to meet a specific commitment. It can be going to the local shop, going out with family or friends, or anything that we need to do. It doesn't matter if the event is five minutes or five months away. The anticipation of having to go beyond our invisible boundaries means breaking our tenuous control of our overall defence. This triggers thoughts of, 'What if . . .?'

What if . . .
- I have a panic attack?
- I can't get help?
- I lose control?
- I faint?
- I lose control of my bladder?
- I have left the stove on?
- I suddenly have to leave?
- I can't get home?
- Everyone sees me shaking?

- I go crazy?
- I have the big one?
- I vomit?
- I make a fool of myself?
- I have an attack of diarrhoea?
- I can't drive?
- People see me this way?
- I let everyone down?
- My face turns bright red?

By the time we need to leave home to meet the commitment, our anxiety level may be so high that we cancel our plans and stay at home. In other words, we avoid the commitment because of a specific spiral of anticipatory anxiety.

Feeling unwell

The third form of avoidance behaviour is scarcely recognised by anyone who does not have one of the disorders. It is the avoidance of situations or places as a result of feeling unwell most of the time. Some people compare this to ongoing flu-like symptoms. We are also continually exhausted, as the anxiety and panic attacks consume all our energy. Going out, going to work or doing normal day-to-day things around the house means not only trying to keep the anxiety and panic attacks at bay, but also trying to overcome the feeling of being unwell and the all-consuming fatigue.

FAMILY MEMBERS

We are not the only ones to be affected by our disorder – it affects our family too. This is not a reason to feel guilty! It isn't our fault that we have developed a disorder. When family members ask what they can do to help their partner, son or daughter recover the first point is for them to take care of themselves first. We all need to take care of ourselves first. This way we can give more effective support and assistance to other people.

Although we may be restricted because of agoraphobia, it is important that our family members live normal lives. I know this can be difficult, because some people with a disorder are unable to be alone. It is a matter of working out a solution that takes into consideration the needs of everyone concerned.

If we will let them, our partner and family members can be of great assistance in helping us learn to develop our mindfulness skills. If we are having an attack or feeling anxious, they can help us to see the thoughts that created it. They can also assist us in working through our avoidance behaviour.

DEPRESSION

As our lives become increasingly restricted through our disorder, many of us develop major depression. The symptoms of depression can be very similar to those of anxiety; this adds to our confusion and we become anxious over our symptoms of depression.

Even today, many people are still not being diagnosed as having an anxiety disorder, and their secondary major depression is assumed to be their primary diagnosis. This only compounds

their confusion even further and can prevent them from accessing
effective treatment for their anxiety disorder.

According to the American Psychiatric Association (1994),
symptoms of depression can include:

- Loss of interest in enjoyable activities
- Irritability
- Changes in appetite
- Lack of concentration
- Insomnia or hypersomnia (oversleeping)
- Fatigue and loss of energy
- Reduction of sexual interest or desire
- Thoughts of suicide

As our lives become more restricted through our anxiety disorder,
we feel helpless in our inability to 'pull ourselves together'. This
only compounds our sense of worthlessness, and some people
can begin to have thoughts of suicide. In some instances, people
feel ashamed of these thoughts and find it extremely difficult to
talk about them. People can also be afraid that if they do talk
about them, they will be committed to hospital.

If you are having thoughts of suicide, don't let feelings of shame
or fears of being committed to hospital stop you from asking for
help. You have nothing to be ashamed of, nor is there anything to
fear by asking for help. It is healthy to do so. Asking for help is
not a sign of weakness or failure. It is an acknowledgement of the
degree of your distress, and you can begin to ease this distress by
asking for assistance. Speak with your doctor. They will understand and be able to assist you.

Talk to your family and tell them how you are feeling. If a family member was feeling this way, you would want to do everything
you could to assist them. You need to give them the opportunity

to be able to assist you. You can also speak with a close friend, your local priest or minister, or you can ring one of the crisis telephone services. You are not alone. Help is available for you. And you can recover.

ALCOHOL

The abuse of alcohol is another form of control, and some people will go on to develop an alcohol dependence. Lack of diagnosis or ineffective treatment has meant that some people use alcohol as a way of 'self-medication', just as they did in our parents' and grandparents' generations, when an anxiety disorder could be 'hidden' behind what was perceived as primarily an alcohol problem.

The use of alcohol as a means of self-medication only perpetuates our panic and anxiety. Most people don't recognise that the symptoms of a hangover are very similar to the feeling of their anxiety disorder. Misinterpreting their hangover symptoms as being either their anxiety or a warning sign of an impending panic attack, they have another drink in an effort to control it, and the cycle continues.

The stigma and shame we all feel about having an anxiety disorder can also be a factor. Quite a number of professional people have told me they think it is more socially acceptable to admit to an alcohol problem than to admit to having an anxiety disorder. An integral part of recovery from an anxiety disorder means that any alcohol problems need to be addressed from the outset.

Another concern is that some people use both prescribed medication and alcohol as a way of trying to control their disorder. This can be dangerous, and it is important for them to speak to their doctor or psychiatrist about it.

CASE HISTORIES

Bill

Bill walked from his manager's office. He knew the day would come when he would be found out and today was that day. He had been caught during working hours in the bar of a hotel, a few doors down from the office. He had been a regular visitor to the hotel, as he made his daily courier rounds to the head office a few blocks away. Having a drink was the way he had found to help him cope with his panic attacks and his perpetual anxiety.

Bill had a regular routine: a drink before going to work, one during his morning round, two at lunch, one on the afternoon round, and two before he drove home. He thought he had at least one thing in his favour: the manager didn't know about his anxiety problems. Bill thought his drinking problem was much more acceptable than having an anxiety problem. What Bill didn't know was that his manager also had the same anxiety disorder.

Michael

The rehabilitation counsellor looked at Michael questioningly. Michael had been on stress leave for eight weeks and was due to return to work the following week. He shifted uncomfortably in his chair. Far from easing his anxiety disorder, Michael was feeling worse. His panic attacks had increased, his anxiety was very high and he was depressed. Every time he left the familiar surroundings of his neighbourhood, he would be overcome with the fear of having another panic attack. The consulting doctor had said Michael was just suffering from stress and that he should think seriously about 'getting his act together' and getting back to work. 'After all,' said the doctor, 'you are lucky to have a job to go back to.'

No one seemed to understand that all Michael wanted to do was to return to work. He certainly didn't like what was happening to him. He had always been conscientious at work and had rarely taken time off. He wondered if he should resign. He thought it would be better than having to face the doubts of his counsellor and his doctor.

SELF-ABSORPTION

Although self-absorption is not a secondary condition, it is another control that many of us use, often without realising it. Our self-absorption will seem to family and friends that we are continually dwelling on our disorder. We are, but not in the way it appears. There is much truth in the statement that 'dwelling on something only makes it worse'. With an anxiety disorder, *not* dwelling on it is almost impossible. We feel as if our lives or our sanity are in constant danger. We feel we may lose control or embarrass ourselves in some way, and so it is extremely difficult not to think about it.

What we don't realise is that the more we worry about it and the harder we try to control it, the worse we get. Not just because we are fighting it. People who have the ability to dissociate can actually induce a dissociated state by becoming self-absorbed. Sometimes our self-absorption can be total. We can be completely focused within ourselves, and without warning we may move into a dissociated state and panic as a result. We get caught up in our fearful 'What if?' cycle of thinking, and round and round we go.

To understand self-absorption, we need to be aware that all people who experience an anxiety disorder, particularly those who are beginning to develop secondary conditions, are caught in an ever-growing maze of anxiety, panic attacks and fear. There appears to be nothing that we or anyone else can do to stop it. The results are totally devastating. Under the circumstances, it is completely normal and natural to become so preoccupied. In fact, not to be preoccupied would be abnormal. The absorption is an attempt to find a way out of our distress. Essentially, we are try-ing to find answers to what appear to be unanswerable questions.

Our absorption is also part of the monitoring process. Monitor-ing each symptom is a way of trying to defend ourselves against them. If we know what our symptoms are 'doing', we feel we won't be taken by surprise in the next minute or the next hour. This is part of our 'early warning' system against further panic attacks and against the 'big one' we feel sure is circling, waiting to strike.

THE NEED TO BE IN CONTROL

There is a final control that forms the basis of all the other controls we use. It can be so subtle that many of us may not be aware of it. It is the *need to be in control*, not only of ourselves but of our whole environment.

The need to be in control permeates every aspect of our life. Before our disorder, our need to be in control assisted us in try-ing to be the 'perfect' person. It assisted us in being able to be all things to all people, to ensure that they thought well of us in any circumstance. With the development of our anxiety disorder, we feel we need to fight harder to be in control as we have already lost so much to the disorder, and we are so afraid of losing control altogether. As a result of our disorder, our need to be in control becomes paramount. Our sense of helplessness and fear demands nothing less. When the anxiety and panic attacks break away from this control, we feel even more helpless than before.

The need to be in control is one of the main obstacles to recovery. Recovery means the opposite. Recovery means we need to let go of the need to be in control. We don't realise that our overwhelming need to be in control perpetuates our disorder. Once we can let go of this particular control, we gain control over our panic and anxiety.

There are various aspects to this particular control, which I discuss in detail in Chapter 10. To let go of this control is unimaginable, but letting go means recovery, and with recovery comes freedom.

CHAPTER 5

Understanding our symptoms

DIAGNOSIS

The symptoms of panic and anxiety can mimic a number of physical conditions, so it is very important to have a full medical check-up to make sure there is no physical cause for these symptoms. Once our doctor has diagnosed panic attacks or anxiety, we need to accept and believe the diagnosis. If not, all we are doing is getting caught up in our fears about them, fuelling the cycle of anxiety and panic (see Chapter 12).

SYMPTOMS

There are infinite combinations of symptoms. I see this in the workshops I run and in speaking with other people who have an anxiety disorder. Some people may have three or four symptoms; others may experience five or six symptoms at any one time. Other people can experience ten or more symptoms at the same time.

Some people report that they have chest pains, palpitations and extreme headaches. Others will have breathing difficulties, diarrhoea, nausea and dizziness. Quite a number of people will have a 'burning red' face, their hands will be visibly shaking and they will perspire profusely. Some people can have all of these symptoms, plus others as well!

Many of us fear our panic attacks overall, while other people may focus on one or two of their panic attack symptoms. Some may fear their breathing difficulties; others will focus on their chest pain and palpitations or missed heartbeats; other people may focus on the fear of having an attack of diarrhoea. Some people will have all of these symptoms but worry about something happening in their lives or what they think should happen, shouldn't happen, could happen, must happen!

Most people who have panic disorder experience dissociative phenomena such as derealisation or depersonalisation. People who have post-traumatic stress disorder can also experience dissociation.

Some people aren't frightened of their dissociative symptoms but worry about their racing heartbeat. Other people will not be frightened of heart palpitations but will be frightened by their dissociative symptoms.

In addition to the experience of depersonalisation and derealisation, many people will feel dizzy and they may feel as if they are going to faint. Some people talk about a tingling, burning sensation, or an electric shock, or a feeling of ice-cold heat moving through their body. And, of course, people can have a racing heart, breathing difficulties, shaking, trembling and a variety of other anxiety symptoms as well as the dissociative ones.

Don't we get confused with our symptoms? They can swap, change, come back, disappear and then reappear with a slight variation. There is a study that shows people with panic disorder can have different symptoms with every single panic attack (Kenardy et al, 1988). And our research also shows this (Arthur-Jones &

Fox, 1994). This is part of the reason why we need to have a very good understanding of our panic attacks and our anxiety. Otherwise we will continue to get caught up in it all. And that only creates more symptoms!

I often say in my workshops that, as we seem to be rid of one symptom, ten more are queuing up waiting to take its place. It is as if the symptoms are standing at the starting gate jumping up and down saying, 'Pick me! Pick me! It's my turn!'.

Working towards our recovery means we need to understand the various symptom groups. In most treatment programs there is usually no distinction made between these groups, which can cause confusion and make it much harder for us to work with our symptoms.

In my workshops, I separate the symptoms into five categories. This enables everyone to understand how their symptoms are being created, which in turn allows individuals to specifically target their particular symptoms and learn to control them more effectively.

Fight and flight response

The first group of symptoms are a result of the 'fight and flight response', a natural reaction in human and animals that automatically activates in times of danger. It enables us to either stay and fight the danger, or to run from it.

Within moments of us perceiving a dangerous situation, the fight and flight response releases adrenaline and other hormones into our body, providing us with the energy we need to deal with the threat. Our heart rate increases, our breathing increases, our muscles tense, we begin to perspire. This is the fight and flight response in action.

When we have an anxiety disorder, we activate the fight and

flight response by the way we are perceiving and thinking about our fears or symptoms. Although we may see these as being dangerous, they aren't. But our body can't tell the difference between our 'What if . . .?' thoughts and the thought, 'Here comes a truck that's lost its brakes, and is heading straight for me.' Our body is doing what it is 'programmed' to do in times of danger.

The problem is that we are creating the threat of danger by the way we think. The more we become caught up in our fears, the more our body responds to the threat of 'here comes that truck', and round and round we go.

Hyperventilation

The second category of symptoms leads in from the fight and flight response. The effects of our rapid breathing can lead to hyperventilation, which is a decrease of carbon dioxide in the bloodstream. This can be experienced as pins and needles in our fingers and hands, feet and around our mouth. We may also feel faint or dizzy. We can become frightened of these symptoms, and our body responds to our thoughts of 'here comes the truck again' and we continue to go round and round!

I meet few people who have actually fainted. A small number of people have told me they have occasionally fallen to the floor, but even then they have never lost consciousness. Even if that does happen, there is no reason to be alarmed. Fainting can be seen as the body's way of getting us and our fearful thinking out of its way, so our breathing can return to normal. It is important to note that if you haven't yet fainted or fallen to the floor as a result of your panic and anxiety, then you probably never will. If it were going to happen it would have been during the initial stages of your disorder.

Hyperventilation is not dangerous. Carbon dioxide levels can be increased simply by cupping our hands over our mouth and nose and breathing into them, and then breathing back the exhaled breath. This is a variation on the most common technique for easing hyperventilation – breathing into a paper bag. Yet I can't help but wonder about this method – we are all frightened of what other people will think of us, and pulling out a paper bag and breathing into it in the office or shopping centre would probably cause us to hyperventilate further!

In the 1980s there was a theory that hyperventilation was the actual cause of panic attacks, but it is now accepted that while hyperventilation can be experienced as part of the overall symptoms, it is not the cause.

Muscle tension

The third group of symptoms are also a result of the fight and flight response. Our muscles tense in preparation either to run from the danger or to stay and fight it. We can experience this in a number of ways: as chest pain, left arm pain, jaw pain, pain in our legs and as extremely painful tension in our neck and head. And when we fear these symptoms, our body responds to the threat of the 'truck' and away we go again!

CASE HISTORIES

Peter
Peter sat on the side of the hospital bed. He was being discharged after spending the night in hospital, having gone there

the night before because he thought he was having a heart attack. After extensive tests, the specialist had told him he had not had a heart attack but a panic attack. Peter had tried to tell the specialist that he had panicked about his symptoms. He had felt terrible and thought he was going to die. 'I don't understand how my symptoms could just be a panic attack. It makes no sense,' he told the specialist.

Suyin

Suyin was thirty when she had her first panic attack. She was sitting in the staff room during her morning coffee break. Without any warning, everything seemed unreal. It was as though she was looking through a white mist. She looked at her hands and they seemed unreal. Her heart began to race and she felt it was skipping beats. She felt as if she was going to be sick, and was overwhelmed with a feeling of wanting to run.

'Are you alright, Suyin,' asked a colleague. 'You are as white as a ghost.'

'I feel very strange,' Suyin replied, trying to keep the anxiety out of her voice. 'I think I need to see my doctor.'

Dissociation

The fourth group of symptoms are a result of dissociation, also known as 'altered states of consciousness' or trance states. This group of symptoms are experienced by people who have panic disorder or post-traumatic stress disorder.

While the ability to dissociate is not taken into account in most theories about anxiety disorders, many people with panic disorder report that the experience of dissociative symptoms is the reason why they panic. This is confirmed in our research (Arthur-Jones & Fox, 1994), in the responses I receive from people when I'm running workshops, and from the many emails I receive via my website.

The more 'distinguishable' sensations of trance states include:

- Derealisation: a feeling as if we or our surroundings are not real, as though we are looking through a white or grey mist or 'veil'
- Depersonalisation: feeling detached from the body, an 'out of body' experience where people feel as if they are above, behind or standing alongside themselves

Other sensations can include:

- Feelings of floating
- Feeling as if our body has expanded
- Feeling as if our body has become smaller
- Feeling as if we are falling into a void
- Oversensitivity to sound; everyday sound and noise is amplified
- Oversensitivity to light, including daylight; increase in depth and brightness of colours
- Oversensitivity to taste
- Oversensitivity to smell
- Oversensitivity to touch
- Visual distortions such as stationary objects appearing to move

No wonder so many of us who dissociate think we are going insane!

One of the effects of the alteration in consciousness is a feeling of dizziness, and there is no doubt that those of us who dissociate can experience quite severe dizziness at times. A research paper that links dizziness to depersonalisation theorises that it is not so much what we are doing at the time we dissociate as 'the magnitude of the change' of consciousness that is significant (Fewtrell & O'Connor, 1988).

The ability to dissociate

The ability to dissociate usually begins in childhood. Some people with an anxiety disorder have a history of childhood abuse, and the ability to dissociate enabled them to 'escape' from this abuse. People who do not have a background of abuse learnt to dissociate in other situations, such as being bullied at school or during lessons that they were not interested in, disliked or could not cope with.

Evidence suggests that people with the ability to dissociate 'may display high hypnotisability and high dissociative capacity' (APA, 1994). While some people are aware of their ability to dissociate, and have always been aware of it, others 'lose' this ability as they grow older. In times of stress this ability can be reactivated, not so much as an 'escape mechanism' but as a result of becoming more vulnerable to the ability to dissociate as a result of the stress.

When we are stressed we can skip meals or not feel like eating at all, and we can have difficulty sleeping. This in turn increases our vulnerability to dissociate and one day, without warning, we do! It is interesting to note that other cultures use fasting and sleep deprivation, among other methods, to deliberately induce various trance states. A leading expert in altered states, Dr Charles Tart, has commented that many other cultures 'believe that almost every normal adult has the ability to go into a trance state' (Tart, 1972). The American Psychiatric Association notes that the states can be an 'accepted expression of cultural or religious experience in many societies' (APA, 1994).

We can unknowingly induce these states by staring – at a book or computer screen, at the road ahead of us when we are driving, at a traffic light or at the car in front of us, or when we are talking with another person. We can stare out of our office window, or as we are walking we can stare at a point in the distance. Essentially we do this any time we find our gaze becoming fixed on something. Fluorescent lights can also induce these states, which is the reason why so many of us can have difficulties in major shopping centres. Intense concentration or deep self-absorption can also be a triggering factor for dissociation.

Nocturnal panic attacks

It is interesting to note that research suggests that a 'sleep panic attack' occurs during the transition from stage two to stage three sleep (Uhde, 1994) – in other words, during an alteration of consciousness. Many people who dissociate report that they can also experience an attack as they begin to go to sleep. This first stage of sleep is called the hypnogogic state.

The hypnogogic state can be accompanied by 'sensory shocks', which can also occur during the transition from dreaming sleep. First noted in 1890, these 'sensory shocks' have been described by researchers as 'an upward surge of indescribable nature, an electric sort of feeling ascending from the abdomen to the head sometimes followed by bodily jerks, or a violent explosion and/or a flash of light' (Oswald, 1962).

Researchers also noted that a 'sense of alarm, together with a cold sweat, laboured breathing and tachycardia (rapid heartbeat) often follow' (Oswald, 1962). And for many of us, this 'sense of alarm' can also describe our feelings of panic.

Sensory shocks

Whether we are awake or asleep, these 'sensory shocks' can also be experienced in conjunction with our dissociative symptoms. From our research (Arthur-Jones & Fox, 1994) it does appear that these 'shocks' are induced by dissociative states.

These sensory shocks are experienced as moving through the body as:

- An electric current
- A rush of unusually intense energy
- Intense burning heat
- Burning, tingling heat
- A wave-like motion
- A hot prickly sensation
- 'Ants crawling' sensation
- Intense cold
- Intense burning cold heat

Many of us panic as a result of these sensations, and the fight-or-flight response is activated. Our study found that 71 per cent of people who experienced this type of attack reported that they found it difficult to link the sensations to that of adrenaline and the fight-or-flight response. The study also showed that 69 per cent of people with panic disorder reported that they experienced an attack while going to sleep, and 86 per cent reported that an attack woke them from sleep. Seventy-eight per cent of people with panic disorder reported experiencing their attacks when they were feeling relatively 'calm' – while watching television, reading a book or relaxing with friends (Arthur-Jones & Fox, 1994).

The behavioural school of thought presupposes that when people are relaxed, they have more time to worry about the symptoms. Not necessarily! When some people are relaxed it is very easy for them to dissociate. One researcher noted that the transition into a trance state can occur in a split-second (Putman, 1989), and it is in that split-second that we can go from feeling relaxed to total panic.

In another study, researchers were surprised to discover a 'paradoxical positive correlation between increases in slow [brain] wave EEG and increasing anxiety' while the patient was at rest (Knott, 1990). 'Slow wave activity' indicates a very relaxed state, so the question becomes: how can we be relaxed and anxious at the same time? The study concluded that 'replication of increases in slow wave activity in further studies would suggest psychobiological disturbances in panic disorder are not merely normal emotions expressed in inappropriate context' (Knott, 1990).

Everyone with panic disorder is well aware that the symptoms of their attacks are not 'merely normal emotions expressed in inappropriate contexts'. By 'normal emotions', the researchers are referring to the fight and flight response.

We all know exactly what the fight and flight response feels like. People who have a history of childhood abuse have felt in danger on many occasions because of that abuse. As adults, many of us with panic disorder have had occasions where we have been in danger; a 'near miss' while driving is a common example.

While the fight and flight response is activated moments after we experience an attack, there is no comparison between the precipitating symptoms of our attacks and the fight and flight response. They are two separate events, albeit moments apart. While this separation is not noted in the theories for anxiety disorders, or in the various treatment options, it has been noted by internationally recognised anxiety disorder specialists.

One psychiatrist (Hafner, 1986) quotes a patient's description of her panic attacks as beginning with a 'tingling feeling going up my spine which enters my head and causes a sensation of faintness and nausea. I feel I'm going to lose control or lose consciousness. I thought I was going to die and started to panic.'

Another psychiatrist describes the attack as being associated with a 'rushing sensation of a hot flash surging through the body' (Sheehan 1983). People can experience the sensation as 'sometimes associated with a sick feeling and a sensation of fading out from the world'. This faintness is more like a 'whiteout' than a 'blackout' and the head may literally 'feel light'. The fear of this attack is then followed by the fight-or-flight response (Sheehan, 1983). Note the separation between the 'attack' and the feelings of panic in both examples.

Dr Clare Weekes (1992) likened the attack to a white-hot flame starting 'just below the breast bone, passing through the chest, up the spine, into the face, down the arms and even down to the groin and to the tips of the toes'. Although Dr Weekes does not separate the 'white hot flame' from the fight-or-flight response, her description is similar to the two previous examples. Nor are there any of the usual fight-or-flight symptoms in her description.

This separation between the 'attack' and the panic is very important, and holds the key to recovery for so many of us. I teach people who experience these types of attacks to learn to separate their dissociative symptoms and any accompanying 'sensory shocks' from their thoughts and feelings of panic and anxiety about them. I discuss this in Chapter 12.

The effects

The fifth group of symptoms are the effects we feel as a result of our anxiety disorder and, in some cases, depression.

Inability to concentrate

Many of us can experience what appears to be a severe loss of concentration. I say 'appears' because our concentration can be all-encompassing and absorbing, but we just don't realise it. Our internal 'radar' is usually constantly scanning for signs of the next attack, the next symptom, the next nasty surprise! At the same time, we take our intellectual understanding to its limit by trying to work out what is happening to us and how we can stop it.

When we try to concentrate on whatever it is we are doing, we find it difficult. Unknowingly, we draw our concentration back into ourselves so that we can keep on 'scanning', and then we become more anxious because we think we can't concentrate!

Sleeping difficulties

We may experience sleeping difficulties. We may not be able to sleep; we may sleep fitfully; we may wake up with a nocturnal panic attack; we may wake in the early hours of the morning and not be able to go back to sleep. We feel the lack of sleep in the heaviness of our head and body, and it is as if we need to 'drag' ourselves around. And, of course, the more we worry about this and our sleeping difficulties, the less sleep we will have and so the effects continue.

Loss of feelings and loss of libido

Two of the most distressing effects are what appears to be the loss of feelings towards our partner, children, family and friends. We can also experience a loss of libido. While the loss of libido can be a side effect of antidepressants, people who are not using them also report this effect.

If we look at our overall experience, and our various fears, we can begin to see how our loss of feelings occur. Many of us feel as if we are fighting to survive, fighting to stay sane, fighting not to lose control or embarrass ourselves in some way. As a result, we simply don't have the energy or 'space' to feel anything else. Obviously, we become anxious over our loss of feelings, and this keeps it keeping on.

Fatigue

Sleeping difficulties can leave us feeling exhausted. Those who don't have these difficulties can also feel completely exhausted every waking moment. Again, if we look at our overall experience, it becomes clear that we are using so much energy. The fight-or-flight response can be continually activated as we fight our anxiety and panic, sometimes each moment of the day. Is it any wonder we feel so exhausted?

Appetite problems

If we are not eating, or if we are eating very lightly, we can also feel physically weak. We may be feeling too nauseous or too unwell to eat. We can feel light-headed, dizzy, shaking or trembling, and we may have a headache. We can lose weight. Usually, we don't recognise these effects for what they are – an effect of not eating – and so we worry about them, and they join the ever-expanding panic and anxiety cycle.

In essence, the effects of our anxiety disorder create more anxiety and panic, which in turn increases our anxiety, which compounds the effects.

New symptoms

As we move through the recovery process, our symptoms will swap and change. This can be frustrating as well as frightening.

It is important that we speak to our doctor about any new symptoms. I know people hesitate because they think they have hypochondria, but we do need to speak to our doctor. If not, we can spend weeks worrying about the new symptom instead of working through it. And obviously, we need to know that any new symptom is part of our anxiety disorder!

To help ease thoughts about hypochondria and our feelings of embarrassment, we can ask our doctor to work in partnership with us. We can tell our doctor that we are working through to recovery, and that we need their assistance to enable us to work with any new symptom rather than becoming caught up in further anxiety and panic about it.

Overlapping symptoms

Use the check list below to help you to understand how your symptoms are being created. Some symptoms can overlap into other groups. For example, the physical responses to not eating properly include dizziness and feeling light-headed. These symptoms can also belong to the hyperventilation group as well as the dissociative group.

Not eating properly can also make us more vulnerable to dissociation, and if we dissociate we may experience additional symptoms of dizziness and light-headedness. We may panic or become anxious about these symptoms and then hyperventilate, which can create similar symptoms yet again.

Is it any wonder that we get confused! The more mindful we become, the more we will be able to isolate which of these groups of symptoms we are experiencing. Then we can learn how to turn them off!

If we dissociate, we need to be aware of how we are inducing trance states. Are we staring, under fluorescent light, or deeply absorbed in our thoughts? We can break the trance state by taking a deep breath, by blinking or by letting go of the absorption in our thoughts. I discuss this in detail in Chapter 12.

Many of our symptoms come from the fight-or-flight response. We can turn off these symptoms by learning to manage our panic and anxiety thinking. As we learn to manage our attacks and anxiety, the effects we experience as a result of our disorder dissipate.

Symptom check list

DISSOCIATIVE SYMPTOMS

☐ Derealisation: feelings that you and/or your surroundings are not real; experience your surroundings through a diffused light, fog or mist

☐ Depersonalisation: feeling detached from your body

☐ Feeling as if you are floating

☐ Feeling as if your body has expanded

☐ Feeling as if your body has become smaller

☐ Feeling as if you are falling into a void

☐ Tunnel vision

☐ Oversensitivity to sound; everyday sounds are amplified

☐ Oversensitivity to light and colours; an increase in the depth and brightness of colours

☐ Oversensitivity to taste

☐ Oversensitivity to smell

☐ Oversensitivity to touch

☐ Visual distortions; stationary objects appear to move or sway

☐ Feeling 'spacey'

- [ ] Feeling surreal
- [ ] Dizziness
- [ ] Light-headedness
- [ ] Feeling as if you are going to faint

SENSATIONS THAT MAY ACCOMPANY DISSOCIATIVE SYMPTOMS
- [ ] 'Electric current' moving through the body
- [ ] Rush of unusually intense energy moving through the body
- [ ] Intense burning heat moving through the body
- [ ] Burning, tingling heat moving through the body
- [ ] Wave-like motion moving through the body
- [ ] Hot, prickly sensation moving through the body
- [ ] 'Ants crawling' sensation moving through the body
- [ ] Intense cold sensation moving through the body
- [ ] Intense cold burning heat sensations moving through the body

FIGHT-OR-FLIGHT RESPONSE
- [ ] Racing heartbeat
- [ ] Heart palpitations
- [ ] Missed heartbeats (ectopic)
- [ ] Rapid shallow breathing
- [ ] Difficulty in breathing
- [ ] Difficulty in taking a deep breath
- [ ] Nausea
- [ ] Burning or churning in the stomach
- [ ] Indigestion
- [ ] Shaking
- [ ] Trembling
- [ ] Diarrhoea
- [ ] Vomiting

☐ Loss of bladder control
☐ Perspiring
☐ Burning red face

HYPERVENTILATION AS A RESULT OF THE FIGHT-OR-FLIGHT RESPONSE

☐ Pins and needles
☐ Feeling light-headed
☐ Feeling dizzy
☐ Feeling faint

MUSCLE TENSION AS A RESULT OF FIGHT-OR-FLIGHT RESPONSE

☐ Chest pain
☐ Left arm pain
☐ Neck ache
☐ Headache
☐ Jaw pain
☐ Leg pain
☐ Choking sensation
☐ Tightening in the throat

EFFECTS

☐ Loss of appetite
  – feeling faint
  – feeling dizzy
  – feeling light-headed
  – shaking and trembling
  – feelings of physical weakness
  – weight loss
☐ Loss of concentration
☐ Extreme exhaustion

- [ ] Loss of feelings towards loved ones
- [ ] Loss of libido
- [ ] Sleeping difficulties
  - feeling heavy-headed
  - headache
  - feeling dazed
- [ ] Flu-like symptoms
- [ ] Sinus problems
- [ ] Earaches
- [ ] Aching joints
- [ ] Left-hand-sided weakness

MAJOR FEARS

- [ ] Feeling as if you are having a heart attack
- [ ] Feeling as if you are going to die
- [ ] Feeling as if you are going insane
- [ ] Feeling as if you are going to faint
- [ ] Making a fool of yourself
- [ ] Embarrassing yourself in some way
- [ ] Going to lose control
  - vomiting
  - diarrhoea
  - loss of bladder control
  - literally losing control

CHAPTER 6

Therapies

In the recent past and even now, many people have tried a number of therapies and treatments with little or no effective outcome. Not only does this contribute to people's general sense of helplessness and hopelessness, it can also generate anger towards the health professions.

If we have had an anxiety disorder for a number of years, we may be angry about the overall lack of understanding about our condition, and about not receiving an earlier diagnosis and effective treatment. Many people who have had the disorder for years feel cheated by the loss of family, social and employment opportunities. There is also anger that our doctors' failure to understand has strengthened the myths and stigma surrounding anxiety disorders. These include that we are weak in character, not trying hard enough, or gaining too many secondary benefits from the disorder to really want to recover.

Now there are effective treatment options available we can use our anger constructively by becoming more proactive. It is up to us as individuals to access as much information as we can about the various treatment options available, and to choose the most effective option that meets our needs. Our recovery demands nothing less.

We can also become more proactive in our choice of doctor or therapist. Many of us accept inadequate treatment because we think we are inadequate. We don't think we have the right to change our doctor or voice our concerns, and then we become angry because we don't receive the help we need.

In some cases we can have misguided loyalty to the doctor, therapist or our family. Although we complain privately, we continue to go to back to our doctor or therapist because we don't want to let our family, doctor or therapist down.

In other cases, family members feel a stronger loyalty to the doctor than we do. Our family pressures us to remain with the doctor, so we stay in a therapy situation that may be of little benefit to us.

THE NEED TO BE PERFECT

Prior to the disorder, many of us were perfectionists and, despite the disorder, we still try to present this image. Not only have we tried to be the perfect partner, the perfect parent, the perfect employee or employer, we now become the perfect patient. Discussing issues where we feel ashamed or humiliated does not fit our 'perfect' image, so we hold back.

I have seen this happen on so many occasions. In many instances we will not tell our doctor or therapist the full effects of what we are experiencing, including thoughts of suicide. I have seen people discharged from treatment because they present the perfect image to their therapist, yet they may be in more difficulty than when they first started treatment. The last thing we need, and the last thing our therapists need, is a perfect patient!

CASE HISTORIES

Lily

Lily called her husband at work and asked him to come home because she was frightened something was going to happen to her. She had been to five different doctors and not one of them had been able to tell her what was wrong with her. Most had said she was just anxious; some had prescribed various tranquillisers or antidepressants. Feeling the way she did was making her anxious. If they could just tell her what was wrong with her and help her, she would stop being anxious. It was beginning to affect her relationship with her husband. She didn't want to bother him at work, but she didn't know what else to do.

Thea

Thea was convinced she would never recover. Five years ago she was diagnosed as having panic disorder and generalised anxiety, yet she had been experiencing it for twenty-five years. Over that time she had seen many doctors, psychiatrists and psychologists, and taken all types of medication, all to little or no avail. A doctor had once commented that she was depressed. She thought it was natural that she was depressed, and wondered why people only treated her depression and not the underlying cause.

At the hospital day clinic her doctor and the nurses would pat her on the shoulder and tell her to 'think positive'. She tried, but it was difficult when her life had disintegrated and there seemed no way she could ever get back to 'normal'.

Thea gave up and refused to see any other doctor or

specialist. She was angry and frustrated at the lack of help, but there seemed to be no solution. Gradually, she was able to arrange her life around her disorder. She could do her own shopping at the local store, but she spent most of her time at home. Her children grew up with the impression that their mother was a bit eccentric, but they had accepted her as she was and never questioned her decision not to seek further help.

One day Thea's daughter was watching a talk show on television. They were discussing anxiety disorders and how the new cognitive techniques were helping people to recover. She looked over at her husband questioningly. 'Ring your mother,' he said, 'it is worth having a word to her about it.'

Chloe

It was Saturday night and Chloe was at home with her parents. Her friends were out celebrating the end of their first year at university. They hadn't understood when Chloe had pulled out of university during the second semester. She had always been a straight-A student. Now she wasn't doing anything at all. She refused all invitations to go out and stayed home most of the time. She went out only occasionally with her parents. Her brother had told her friends that she had always been somewhat shy but for some reason it became worse when she started university. Now she was scared of making a fool of herself when she was around people, including her friends. She refused to see a doctor because she was scared what they would say.

MINDFULNESS AND OTHER COGNITIVE TECHNIQUES

Many of us are aware of the predominant role our thoughts play. This was confirmed in one Australian study of panic disorder (Kenardy et al, 1988) that showed patients had 'a clear bias toward attributing cause to cognitive factors'. As in my experience with clients, the study also showed that people preferred 'cognitive coping strategies' in preference to medication. When medication is used, it does need to be used in conjunction with mindfulness or other cognitive behavioural therapies. We control every aspect of our life except the way we think, yet it is the way we think that is the major contributor to the perpetuation of our anxiety disorders.

Mindfulness as a cognitive technique

Mindfulness is different from other cognitive techniques because it uses mindfulness meditation as its foundation. In meditation, we learn to become aware of our thoughts. We watch and observe our thoughts and associated feeling states, rather than becoming involved in them. Mindfulness as a cognitive technique teaches us to use these skills in everyday life by seeing the cause and effect of our experience – the *cause* being our negative thinking patterns, and the *effects* being our panic, anxiety and other painful feeling states. In seeing this ongoing cause and effect, we learn to lose the fear of our experience and we see we have a choice in what we think about. We can then choose to let go of these thought patterns, and we learn to let our feeling states happen without fighting them, thereby enabling us to gain control over our panic and anxiety.

On a personal note, one of the most valuable aspects of mindfulness as a cognitive technique for me was that it taught me to believe emotionally that nothing was going to happen as a result of my panic and anxiety. We may know intellectually that our panic and anxiety will not hurt us, but emotionally we don't believe it. Recovery means that we need to believe it emotionally.

As our mindfulness skills develop, we can then work on any avoidance behaviour using the mindfulness principles outlined above (see also Chapter 12).

Cognitive behavioural therapy

Cognitive behavioural therapy (CBT) is a series of strategies specifically targeted at our particular disorder. For panic disorder, these strategies can include relaxation, breathing techniques, 'interoceptive exposure' and cognitive therapy. Interoceptive exposure is designed to produce a number of the most common symptoms, including accelerated heart rate, dizziness and the effects of hyperventilation.

In most cognitive programs for anxiety disorders, people are instructed to write down their numerous anxiety- or panic-producing thoughts. They are then asked to question the validity of these thoughts and to write down more realistic thoughts to counter their negative ones.

With cognitive techniques, we can begin to change our fearful interpretation of the symptoms and break the anxiety-producing thoughts. Armed with cognitive behavioural strategies, we can enter situations or places we have been avoiding and 'test' our ability to manage our anxiety and panic attacks.

Using mindfulness or another cognitive behavioural therapy technique requires commitment and discipline. If we want to be able to learn to manage our panic attacks and anxiety ourselves, we need to commit and do the work that is required; otherwise we won't recover. It is a commitment that will give us the opportunity to break the seemingly never-ending cycle of panic and anxiety.

Graded exposure

A cognitive behavioural therapist will normally work with various types of exposure methods pertaining to our particular anxiety disorder. In the recent past, many people were given a graded exposure program without being taught any cognitive skills. Without these skills, graded exposure is simply exposure to situations or places we avoid.

Some graded exposure programs treat the avoidance behaviour in panic disorder as though it was the situation or place that triggered the attacks and anxiety. People who have panic disorder without any form of avoidance behaviour have also sometimes been given a graded exposure program. The question many people ask is, 'Exposure to what?'

The rationale behind these graded exposure programs is that when people put themselves into avoided situations or places and stay in that situation or place, then the anxiety or panic attack will peak and slowly ebb away. In other words, the person will become habituated to the anxiety and panic attack in that situation or place. As many people say, even though the panic attack does subside, as it always does, if they are not directly frightened of the situation or place, why would the anxiety 'ebb away' when it has never done so before. Trying to correct avoidance behaviour without working on the cause achieves only limited success, which can be destroyed by the next panic attack.

One of the main complaints from people with panic disorder is that most of these programs insist that people stay in the situation or place until the anxiety and panic attack subsides. It seems illogical to put yourself in a city mall, or any other place, for hours on end in an effort to reduce anxiety. Many people are chronically anxious day in day out, and are also experiencing ongoing panic attacks. As people with panic disorder often say, if they were going to become habituated to the anxiety and panic attacks, they would have already done so, irrespective of where they were.

To compound the issue and the confusion, many panic disorder clients are asked to list their secondary fears and a graded exposure program is built around them, rather than the fears inherent within a spontaneous attack. In some cases the list of fears includes specific fears which predated the attacks and have no bearing on their disorder. One study showed that 'half the simple (specific) phobias in panic disorder had childhood onset and half had onset associated with the onset of panic disorder' (Argyle et al, 1990). In other words, some of the specific fears predated the attacks yet had become part of the main focus of treatment. The three categories of panic attacks demonstrate quite clearly that a spontaneous panic attack is not triggered by external cues. In panic disorder, treatment needs to be directed to the cause of the spontaneous panic attack and not the secondary fears.

When we begin to work with our avoidance behaviour we will probably feel anxious, and the 'what ifs?' may return. In only a few seconds, the 'what ifs?' can create a mountain of fear and anxiety that seems insurmountable. We may forget any management strategies we have learnt and become caught up in the automatic cycle of thinking. Some people will then delay doing the exposure work and will wait until their anxiety disappears. This is defeating the purpose of doing exposure work! We need to go back into situations and places feeling anxious and panicky. This is how we learn to control it.

MEDICATION

Medication is usually the 'front-line' defence against panic attacks and anxiety. It is often the only treatment option people are offered when they visit their doctor, even if they have only experienced one panic attack. 'While there is a time and place for medication, especially if someone is feeling suicidal, medication by itself is not the definitive long-term answer for many people.' (Otto et al, 1994)

If medication is the only treatment option offered by your doctor, it is very important to ask them about other options such as mindfulness or other cognitive behavioural therapies, which will teach the necessary skills to manage panic attacks and anxiety over the long term. Speak with your doctor and ask them to assist you in formulating a 'mental health plan' that features cognitive behavioural therapy.

Studies show that many people would prefer not to take medication for their anxiety disorder (Arthur-Jones & Fox, 1997; Kenardy et al, 1988). Yet despite their reluctance to use medication, the majority do so, often with little or no knowledge about the medication they are taking. We all have a responsibility to ourselves to become proactive and informed.

When speaking with our doctor about our disorder, we can feel embarrassed and ashamed, and feel we have no right to discuss any questions or concerns we may have in regards to the medication we are being prescribed. This is not so. We have every right to ask, and most people will find the majority of doctors and psychiatrists will be more than willing to answer questions and discuss any concerns.

If we decide to use medication, we need to be able to make an informed decision and know exactly what we are taking. So many people who speak to me have no idea of the type of medication they are using, and don't know if it is a tranquilliser or an anti-depressant. Nor do they have any idea of possible side effects, or withdrawal symptoms or 'discontinuation reactions' (BMJ, 1998).

We need to know the expected short- and long-term outcomes. We need to know how long we will be taking the medication for, and how long it will take for the medication to begin to work; for example, it may take four to six weeks for the full effects of an antidepressant to be felt.

We need to know if there are any potential interactions with other medications, including herbal or other over-the-counter preparations, and any interactions with alcohol. Women considering becoming pregnant or breastfeeding need to know of any possible risk to their baby. When we have this information, we can make a responsible decision in conjunction with our doctor or therapist as to the most suitable treatment for us.

We also need to know about possible side effects and withdrawal symptoms or 'discontinuation' reactions. In some instances, people are being told that their medication has no side effects and/ or potential withdrawal or discontinuation symptoms. If we are told this, we need to check this information for ourselves. We can change doctors or speak with our local pharmacist, or we can access a number of websites that provide this information.

If we do experience side effects, we need to speak with our doctor. Depending upon the side effects and their severity, our doctor may wish us to continue with the medication or they may change it. Occasionally, some people are told it is their anxiety and not the medication that is creating the new symptoms. It is then up to us to either seek a second opinion or to check the possible side effects of the medication ourselves.

Sometimes, people can be taking medication for months or years with little effect. If there is no marked change in our anxiety disorder after being on medication for eight weeks, we need to discuss this with our doctor and ask for our medication to be changed. If we are refused, we need to change our doctor.

If we are told we will need to be on medication for the rest of our life, we need to ask why and ask for a referral to a cognitive behavioural therapist. If we are refused, we need to change our doctor. This can also apply if we are told we will need to be on medication for a year or two before seeing a cognitive behavioural therapist. Again we need to ask why, and then, depending upon the answer, we can seek a second opinion.

Many people become frustrated because they only see their doctor or psychiatrist for ten to fifteen minutes every few weeks to have their prescription renewed. Again, we need to ask for a referral to a cognitive behavioural therapist, and if we are refused, we need to change our doctor.

Some people report that their doctor or psychiatrist doesn't recommend cognitive behavioural therapy, or they are told it is ineffective in the treatment of anxiety disorders. This is another instance when we need to consider changing our doctor, as cognitive behavioural therapy is considered internationally as 'best practice' in the treatment of anxiety disorders.

It is extremely important that we do not skip or forget to take our medication at the prescribed times, as some people may begin to experience withdrawal or discontinuation reactions by missing just one dose. Another equally important point is that we must not suddenly stop taking our medication, as this can be dangerous. If we do want to stop using our medication, we need to speak to our doctor and withdraw slowly under medical supervision.

Tranquillisers

Tranquillisers were one of the first defences against anxiety and panic. Research shows that these drugs can be addictive. While there can be a role for tranquillisers, especially in helping to ease any crisis people may experience at the beginning of their disorder, the guidelines for prescribing tranquillisers is for two to four weeks only (Brayley et al, 1991). This minimises the risk of possible addiction.

Many people are still being prescribed tranquillisers on a long-term basis. If they are using one of the shorter acting tranquillisers, withdrawal symptoms can occur if they do not take their medication at the prescribed time. These withdrawal symptoms can include anxiety and panic attacks. Sometimes these symptoms are attributed to the original disorder and the dosage of medication is increased, leading to further dependency on the medication.

Unfortunately, in some instances people are still being told that tranquillisers are not addictive, or that research shows they are not as addictive as first thought. It is difficult and confusing when we are confronted with these conflicting points of view, but we have a responsibility to ourselves to be able to make an informed decision about whether to use tranquillisers in the long term.

Withdrawal

Part of the recovery process for people who are using tranquillisers means slowly withdrawing their medication under the supervision of their doctor or psychiatrist. Research suggests that cognitive behavioural therapy can be very effective during withdrawal (Otto et al, 1994), and can help us to effectively work through this process.

Antidepressants

Antidepressants are widely used in the treatment of anxiety disorders, with varying degrees of success in keeping the anxiety and panic attacks at bay. While antidepressants can be very useful if we are beginning to think about suicide, like any medication they do not teach us the necessary cognitive skills we need. If we decide to use antidepressants, we can use the time while taking them to learn mindfulness or other cognitive skills. These skills will enable us to control any future panic attacks and anxiety ourselves, once we have withdrawn from the medication.

Withdrawal/discontinuation reactions

Research confirms the possibility that some people may develop 'discontinuation' reactions as they withdraw their antidepressant. These reactions can begin within a short time after the medication has been withdrawn and can last for 'one day to three weeks' (BMJ, 1998). As the discontinuation reactions can include anxiety and panic attacks, it is important that the reaction is not misinterpreted by ourselves or our doctor as being a return of our anxiety disorder. This could lead 'to unnecessary reinstatement of the antidepressant' (BMJ, 1998).

Mindfulness or other cognitive behavioural skills will help us if we experience withdrawal symptoms, and they will also help us to control any future panic attacks or anxiety.

CASE HISTORIES

Patricia

The prescription lay on the table. Will she or won't she have it filled? Years ago Patricia had been given a similar medication. She had never liked the thought of it, but her panic attacks and anxiety finally convinced her she had to do something. It had helped her for a while, but over time she found she had to keep increasing the dose for it to have any effect. Finally, she decided enough was enough and slowly withdrew from the medication. Patricia had learnt to cope with the panic attacks and the anxiety, but over the last two months they had become more and more intense. She didn't want to take the medication, but she thought she had no other option to control her disorder.

If we are prescribed medication, we need to discuss this fully with our doctor. It is *our responsibility to ourselves* to be informed about the medication we are taking. The following check list is based on the most common questions I am asked every day about medication.

Medication check list

- We have the right to discuss any questions and concerns we have about our medication with our doctor
- There is no reason to feel embarrassed or ashamed about this
- If you experience side effects and feel unsure about them, speak with your doctor

- If you are told after commencing medication that any new symptoms are part of your disorder, seek a second opinion

Questions to ask your doctor

- Why is the medication being prescribed, and how does it work?
- What type of medication is being prescribed: tranquilliser, antidepressant or another?
- How long does it take before the medication becomes fully effective?

Tranquillisers

If you are being prescribed tranquillisers, ask:
- How long will you be taking this medication? Be mindful that tranquillisers can become addictive within two to four weeks (Brayley et al, 1991).
- How long before the medication becomes fully effective?
- What are the short- and long-term outcomes?
- What is the exact prescribed dose you are to take each day?
- What are the side effects?
- For what length of time is a single dose effective?
- What are the possible withdrawal effects if a single dose is accidentally missed?
- What are the possible withdrawal effects when discontinuing tranquillisers permanently?
- If there are withdrawal effects, how long will they last?
- If you are told you will need to take tranquillisers for longer than a month, seek a second medical opinion.
- If you are told minor tranquillisers have no side effects at all, or are not addictive, change your doctor.

Antidepressants

If you are being prescribed antidepressants, ask:
- How long will you be taking this medication?
- How long before the medication becomes fully effective? Antidepressants can take up to six weeks.
- What are the short- and long-term outcomes?
- What is the exact prescribed dose you are to take each day?
- What are the side effects?
- For what length of time is a single dose effective?
- What are the possible withdrawal effects if a single dose is accidentally missed?
- What are the possible withdrawal effects when discontinuing antidepressants permanently? (BMJ, 1998)
- If there is a discontinuation reaction, how long will it last?

Using medication

- Antidepressants cannot be used on a casual basis.
- It is our responsibility to take our medication as it has been prescribed.
- To prevent any possible withdrawal or discontinuation reactions, ensure you have a new prescription filled two days before your current prescription runs out.
- Check with your doctor or pharmacist to see if there are any adverse interactions with other prescribed medications or over-the-counter preparations such as cold and flu medication or herbal products.
- Women who are considering pregnancy, who are pregnant or are breastfeeding need to speak with their doctor about any possible risk to their baby.
- Do not use alcohol when taking prescribed medication; speak to your doctor about this.

- Do not stop using your medication. If you are considering stopping your medication, you need to speak with your doctor. Withdrawal of your medication needs to be done gradually over a period of time under medical supervision.

Other

- If you have been taking an antidepressant for over six weeks and you find there is no significant improvement in how you are feeling, discuss this with your doctor and ask for your medication to be changed.
- If you are told you will be on medication for the rest of your life because of your anxiety disorder, change your doctor.
- If you only see your doctor for a minimum amount of time every few weeks, ask for a referral to a cognitive behavioural therapist; if you are refused, change your doctor.
- If you are told cognitive behavioural therapy is not recommended, or your doctor tells you it doesn't work, change your doctor.
- If you are told you will be referred to a cognitive behavioural therapist in six months, or a few years, change your doctor.

CASE HISTORIES

Elizabeth

Elizabeth had panic disorder but she didn't avoid anything. She went to work and did everything she needed to do, but her ongoing anxiety made it difficult. She went to see a specialist, although she had to wait five months for an appointment. When she arrived at the clinic, the specialist was running late because of an emergency. When he eventually arrived, he greeted her with a grunt and a nod of his head as he beckoned her into his office. Although the appointment was scheduled for an hour, he told Elizabeth that it needed to be cut short to twenty minutes.

The specialist asked her what she was frightened of and she told him she was scared and anxious she might die from her attacks. The specialist kept saying that she had to be scared of something, but Elizabeth wasn't sure what he meant. In the end she told him that she had always been scared of elevators, but that was long before the panic attacks started. The specialist told her to go into the foyer, get into an elevator and go up and down in it until her anxiety disappeared. With that he finished the appointment and told her to book another with his secretary. She didn't.

Xavier

The session with Xavier's psychiatrist had not gone well. What had started off as a normal session ended with the psychiatrist telling him that he had made so much improvement, his sessions could be cut back to once a month. Xavier knew he had made a mistake and he walked out of the psychiatrist's office feeling totally devastated. What his psychiatrist didn't know was that Xavier was in fact worse than when he'd first started seeing the psychiatrist.

Two weeks ago Xavier had refused a promotion, as he was already having difficulty with his current job. He thought back to all the times when he hadn't been completely honest with his psychiatrist. He hadn't wanted to explain all the details of what he was experiencing, as he had never met anyone who really understood what was happening to him. He had joined a couple of chat rooms and message boards for people with anxiety disorders on the internet, but he was hesitant. Although their experiences were similar to his, Xavier couldn't stop the thoughts that he was different from everyone else. He was also afraid that if he told the psychiatrist everything, he would be committed to a psychiatric hospital. Xavier wondered if he should ring the psychiatrist and explain everything, but he felt too humiliated and ashamed.

PSYCHOTHERAPY

Psychotherapy has sometimes been the only treatment people have tried. It can be difficult to see the relevance of psychotherapy to anxiety disorders, but if we have a history of childhood abuse or have undergone some other trauma, psychotherapy is very important. Despite the sense of shame many of us feel over these issues, they need to be dealt with for our long-term wellbeing. There are very understanding and caring therapists working in the area of childhood abuse, and the local public hospital or community centre can refer anyone who needs help.

Even if there is no major past or present trauma, psychotherapy, in conjunction with cognitive behavioural therapy, can be extremely beneficial. Many of us who have an anxiety disorder have suppressed our primary emotions of anger, grief and sadness. We don't realise that these emotions can convert to the passive feelings of anxiety and depression. Psychotherapy helps us get in touch with our emotions so we can learn to express them in healthier ways.

Some of us are frightened of psychotherapy in case we find out we are 'really bad' people. This is one of the most common fears associated with psychotherapy, but there is no basis to this fear. We need to take the risk. We will discover there is nothing 'bad' about us. Like everyone else, there will be aspects about ourselves we may not like, but only when we know these aspects can we modify and integrate them. I discuss this further in Chapter 15.

Psychotherapy means more than just looking at the problems and difficulties of childhood. It is not so much a process of who is to blame, as a process of understanding causes and effects. It looks at how we, as children, responded in certain situations. These responses created the defences, motivations and patterns of behaviour that we unconsciously carried into adulthood, but which may not be appropriate now. When we become aware of these responses, we are then able to change them if we want to.

HYPNOTHERAPY

Many of my clients have used hypnotherapy at some point in their disorder. While it may have assisted them at that particular point in time, it did not teach them the necessary cognitive skills they needed for long-term recovery. Gradually, their panic and anxiety returned, sometimes with a vengeance. If hypnosis is used, it needs to be done in conjunction with mindfulness or other cognitive behavioural therapy strategies.

OTHER THERAPIES

In the last few years, a number of other treatment programs for anxiety disorders have been introduced. One such program stated that it could help people with panic disorder get over their fear of open spaces! When considering any treatment program, we need to verify that the program is effective and that the therapists or counsellors have the current knowledge and understanding of anxiety disorders.

Before committing to any treatment program, we need to speak with the therapist or counsellor concerned. We have the right to ask them about their experience in treating people with anxiety disorders, and how long they have been doing so. We also have the right to ask them for copies of their research which demonstrates the effectiveness of their treatment program. Our mental health demands nothing less!

AN OVERVIEW

When we look at the list of therapies available, it can be quite overwhelming. However, it isn't as daunting as it looks. Understanding of the disorders has come a long way, and for many of us freedom from the disorders is a reality.

Cognitive behavioural therapy and medication, either used together or individually, are 'best practice' in the treatment of anxiety disorders. Treatment programs which incorporate relaxation, breathing techniques and cognitive behavioural therapy have been associated with dramatic success (Otto et al, 1994). A program, conducted in Queensland, that used similar methods showed 'long term improvements', which is not only beneficial for people with the disorder as it 'quickly restores functioning', but is also 'cost effective' (Evans, 1995). This is an important issue in any treatment service that cannot be ignored.

Treatment programs that do not assist us in learning how to manage our panic attacks and anxiety through a cognitive technique need to be questioned. Only *we* can change our thought patterns. No one can do this for us.

Recovery is a step-by-step process. While mindfulness or other cognitive skills are the most important techniques, short-term medication may be required; conversely, if drug or alcohol dependence is involved, this will also need to be worked with. After our cognitive skills are sufficiently developed and our life is coming back on track, we may want to address any outstanding personal issues by seeing a skilled psychotherapist. The secret is to use the various therapies we need when we need them. Combined together, we can take the power back.

Part 2

Prelude to recovery

CHAPTER 7

Simply not me

ALL THINGS TO ALL PEOPLE

Even before our anxiety disorder developed, we did not know
or feel any sense of self, any sense of who we are. Our identity is
based on the roles we assume in our life. We are a wife, husband,
father, mother, daughter, son, friend, work colleague. We are a
nurse, carpenter, truck driver, school teacher, receptionist, waiter,
company executive, secretary. Our identity is based on our own,
and other people's, expectations and perceptions of who we think
we should be. We think we need to be all things to all people,
so that people will love us. To accomplish this, we suppress our
feelings, needs and wants – in essence, ourselves. As a result, our
sense of self is 'externally' based rather than centred within us.

Trying to be all things to all people takes an enormous amount
of energy. It also takes an enormous amount of strength to continually hold ourselves back, to not show our feelings and not feel
our feelings. To always be pleasant, smiling and helpful. To take
responsibility for everyone else, and to make sure we do all the
above perfectly!

While we can have the love of our partner, family and friends, many of us know the sense of disquiet within us. That we are not who we appear to be. We feel inferior and we worry that we will be 'found out' and exposed as being less than perfect.

As our anxiety disorder develops, we are thrown back within ourselves, and we feel as if there is nothing there to give us the strength and support we need. There is. We just don't recognise it or know how to find it. The development of a sense of self is an ongoing process throughout our lives. Unknowingly, we have stopped this process, and in doing so we have been unable to develop a sense of self. A sense of who we are.

Intellectually and physically, we have matured, but emotionally we are still relating to people and the world around us as we did in childhood. This is not to say we are childish; it means we have never learnt to express our own thoughts, emotions, ideas and creativity. In essence, these are the building blocks of our sense of self and identity. Without them there is no internal frame of reference, and our self-esteem and sense of worth are centred on other people's perception of us.

Many of us are able to see the difference between our intellectual understanding and our emotional understanding. This is particularly so in relation to our anxiety disorder. We may realise at an intellectual level that our panic attacks and anxiety will not hurt us, but emotionally we struggle with this understanding and continually become caught up in our panic and anxiety fears.

This is why it is so important that we understand on an emotional level why we have nothing to fear from our attacks and our anxiety. When we can do this, we recover. And if we continue to allow our emotional development to unfold, not only will we recover but our identity will become centred within ourselves. We are then safe within ourselves to be ourselves, instead of being who we think we should be.

SELF-ESTEEM

There is very little recognition of the importance of the role that self-esteem plays in the recovery process from an anxiety disorder. From my experience in working with so many people who have a disorder, it is one of the key components to permanent recovery. Healthy self-esteem and anxiety disorders are mutually exclusive. With a healthy sense of self, there is no separation between our intellectual and emotional understanding. And this integrated understanding cannot be dissolved, either by panic attacks or anxiety.

I have always taught that recovery from an anxiety disorder is the loss of fear of our attacks, our anxiety and our fears. Lose the fear and we lose the disorder. When we first develop panic and anxiety, we perceive them to be life threatening or a threat to our sanity, or a sign that we are about to lose control in some way. In reality, they are panic attacks or symptoms of high anxiety. Nothing more.

There is no dispute that the symptoms can feel very severe, but they will not hurt us in the ways we think they will. We may know this intellectually, but emotionally we don't. Emotionally it is the way that we perceive them and think about them that causes the harm. And it this perception that can harm us to the point that it can destroy our lives as we knew them to be.

CASE HISTORIES

A group discussion

'I don't have low self-esteem,' Jackie said to the group leader. 'Before having panic disorder, I was the life of the party, I was really extroverted.'

'Me too,' said Melinda.

'And me,' echoed Mark.

'And I think that you would also have a great sense of humour, that you love making people laugh, even at the expense of yourself,' the group leader replied to the three of them.

'Yes.' 'You are right.' 'How did you know that?' they replied.

'It can be part of the personality profile for people with panic disorder,' the leader said. 'But that doesn't necessarily mean you have high self-esteem.'

'It can be a mask that you wear,' Sherry said shyly. 'I have social anxiety and I hide within myself, but you guys are probably hiding behind the extroversion.'

Some of the group seemed surprised by Sherry's comments and everyone turned to the group leader for his response. 'Good insight, Sherry,' he replied. He could see that some of the group wanted to debate the point. 'Let's look at it another way,' he said, forestalling their comments. 'How many in the group are perfectionists?' Everyone nodded as they raised their hands. 'How many in the group wear various masks, being who you think you should be?' Again people nodded and raised their hands. Some in the group needed to think about the question and then somewhat hesitantly raised their hands.

'It's not high self-esteem, is it?' Jackie asked somewhat defensively.

'No, it isn't,' replied the group leader gently. 'And speaking of "no", who has trouble saying no?' Everyone nodded in agreement.

'Healthy self-esteem,' said the group leader, 'is the ability to be able to be ourselves in all situations. To be able to say what we think and to be able to feel what we feel. To be able to honour and respect our thoughts, feelings and emotions no matter the circumstance. Perfectionist behaviour, wearing the masks, saying yes when we mean no, is not accepting ourselves. Nor is it being responsible for ourselves. And this is what causes much of our anxiety and panic.'

We are very passive people, and this is demonstrated in our passivity towards our disorder. Although we constantly fight our panic and anxiety, we do so in ways that only perpetuate them. As our fears can be all-consuming, we are unable to take a more proactive approach and meet our panic and anxiety head-on. When our sense of self is centred within us, we are able to draw upon all of our inner resources and go beyond our fears. This enables us to take a more effective and dominant stand against them.

THE 'ONION'

As I noted in my introduction, recovery is much like peeling an onion. As we work through the recovery process and peel away the layers, we discover these inner resources within us, and we find they have been there all along. We just didn't know it!

Often people with an anxiety disorder will tell me they are weak people and that having an anxiety disorder shows how weak they are. This is not true. Some people have lived with an anxiety disorder for up to fifty years before they were diagnosed or received effective treatment. Living with an anxiety disorder for a few months, let alone fifty years, is an extraordinary demonstration of strength. We are very strong people; in fact, we are too strong for our own good! We simply don't recognise how strong we are. But we will discover this during the recovery process.

When we begin to work towards recovery, we work directly on the immediate cause of our distress. This, of course, is our panic attacks and anxiety, and the many and varied fears we have in relation to them. As we become more aware and skilled in mindfulness and our ability to manage our attacks and anxiety, we begin to see another layer of thoughts and fears besides the obvious 'loud' ones of our disorder.

We begin to see how we relate to ourselves and to other people. We see that in almost everything we do, we seek approval from everyone, no matter who they are – even the stranger standing next to us in a queue! We also see how these fears about what people think of us now generate so much of our underlying anxiety and panic.

THE CREATED SELF

We *do* believe that there is something fundamentally wrong with us, and we *do* fear that we will be rejected or abandoned. These fears have been carried over from childhood, along with the behaviours we adopted as children to prevent these fears from being realised. As we have never addressed and resolved these fears, we are still trying to appease them with behaviours that block our emotional development, which in turn generates our low self-esteem.

Created self	Real self
Low self-esteem	Healthy self-esteem
Not accepting of self	Accepting of self
Saying yes when we mean no	Saying no when we mean no
Taking responsibility for everyone	Being responsible for ourselves
Taking care of everyone	Taking care of ourselves
Trying to please everyone	Pleasing ourselves in how we care for ourselves
Being responsible for other people's happiness	Being responsible for our own happiness
Taking care of other people's feelings	Taking care of our own feelings
Solving other people's problems	Solving our own problems
Meeting other people's wants and needs	Meeting our own wants and needs
Anticipating people's needs before they are aware of them	Anticipating our own needs
Being available to others twenty-four hours a day	Being available to ourselves
Constantly feeling guilty	Recognising why there is no need to feel guilty
Feeling trapped and suffocated by the above	Feeling free
Trying to do all of the above perfectly	Accepting that we are human
Wondering why we have an anxiety disorder	Knowing why we did

Do you recognise yourself in either of these lists? Most people with an anxiety disorder will identify themselves as having low self-esteem. And looking at this list, is it any wonder that we have an anxiety disorder? In one way or another, this is our daily list of things to do, and we need to ask ourselves how much strength does this take? It takes a considerable amount, which is why I always say we are too strong for our own good!

I realise that some people will look at the list for low self-esteem and wonder why this is being called into question. After all, this is how we have been taught to relate to other people. But now, as adults, the behaviours we learnt in childhood are placing us under enormous unnecessary stress and pressure.

As children we were dependent on the love and security of our parents, however tenuous that may have been. For a variety of reasons, however innocuous, we learnt as children that the expression of our self and our feelings was counterproductive to our need to be loved, to 'belong'. As children, we perhaps didn't have the intellectual development to understand the full meaning of the injunctions, demands and expectations placed upon us. We learnt, sometimes very quickly, that it was not in our best interest to be, or to express, ourselves. In response to this, we created a self based upon our interpretation of who and how we should be. We became the 'good nice' child and the 'good nice' adult.

If we come from an abusive background, there is no doubt that these injunctions and demands would have been continually reinforced by this abuse. But even when these statements were counterbalanced by messages of love and caring, the negative messages had much more impact. If the messages of love came after we were 'trying to be good', it only reinforced our conclusion that there was something very wrong with us that we needed to hide. If people were going to love us, we felt we had no choice but to be who we thought they wanted us to be. With fear, shame and confusion, we kept on trying to be good, so that people didn't find out who we really were.

OUR EMOTIONS

We learnt that our anger was not appropriate, and so we suppressed these feelings – to the degree that some of us have reached the point where any feelings of anger 'magically' disappear without us having any, or only partial, awareness of them. This results in our passivity, which is then carried into our passive response to our anxiety disorder.

Our disorder can destroy our lives as we knew them, yet any anger we may feel is directed towards ourselves. If it is directed at our disorder, however, we can make great strides in our recovery. Many people are frightened of any expression of their anger, even towards their disorder. They don't recognise that anger directed towards their disorder is a normal, natural, healthy response.

We also learnt that expressions of sadness and grief were not appropriate, especially if we are men or eldest daughters, and we suppressed these feelings, as we suppressed our anger. This also applies to our spontaneity and our creativity, our intuition and our joyfulness. Again, for a variety of reasons, these were not considered appropriate, and so, like our anger and grief, we suppressed them.

We became the 'good nice' person and good nice people develop anxiety disorders! While there is nothing wrong per se in being good and nice, this is not a spontaneous expression of ourselves. It is an image we needed to create, because we learnt to think that the spontaneous expression of ourselves was wrong.

Instead of learning self-responsibility for our thoughts, feelings and emotions, we assumed responsibility for other people's feelings. Instead of learning to express our own opinions, we learnt to accept other people's opinions as being the truth. Instead of learning to care for ourselves, we took care of everyone else.

We tried to become the perfect child, the perfect student. As we grew, we tried to become the perfect friend, spouse, partner, parent, employee or employer. We became the strong one, the one to whom everyone could bring their problems, their doubts, their fears, their wants and needs. We always tried so hard to please others, even when we may not have liked them, because we needed their approval and we needed them to like or love us.

Our fear of rejection and abandonment has always been there, and is the motivation for all that we do, even now as adults. We feel 'fraudulent' and we worry that one day we will be exposed for not being who everyone thought we were. This fear comes as a direct result of our need to 'create' a self who can please all people, all of the time. In creating this self, we have suppressed our real self, and in this suppression we have rejected and abandoned ourselves.

The process of recovery enables us to reconnect back to ourselves. The practice of mindfulness enables us to manage and control our panic attacks and anxiety. It also allows our emotional development to unfold at a pace we feel comfortable with. As we do, we learn how to treat ourselves with kindness and dignity. We learn to understand and accept ourselves as we are. We learn that taking responsibility for our lives is healthy and extremely empowering, enabling us to become all we could be. We learn to feel our feelings, and we learn how to express them. We also learn to recognise and draw on our own strength. Put these all together, and our anxiety disorder doesn't stand a chance!

CHAPTER 8

Skilful compassionate action

THE CONFLICT

In his book *The Six Pillars of Self-Esteem*, Nathaniel Branden says that 'self-acceptance is my refusal to be in an adversarial relationship to myself' (Branden, 1994).

Unknowingly, we are in an adversarial relationship with ourselves. Our lack of acceptance of ourselves, and our lack of kindness, care and respect for ourselves, is part of this inner conflict. Self-acceptance and self-responsibility are pivotal to the recovery process, and the 'pivot' itself is compassion for ourselves. If we don't accept ourselves, how can we expect our anxiety to disappear? If we are being responsible for other people, and not ourselves, how can we recover? We are not able to recover because not accepting ourselves, not being responsible for ourselves, is creating so much unnecessary anxiety and suffering. This is not a skilful way to live our life.

Let me clarify how I am using the word 'responsibility'. We are a very responsible group of people. In fact, we are too responsible! We have always needed to be all things to all people, to ensure they liked or loved us. Needing to be all things to all people, taking on their problems, being responsible for their happiness and other feelings, means we completely ignore ourselves.

We are perfectionists in everything we do. We go above and beyond the call of duty. A psychiatrist once commented that if an employer hired five people with an anxiety disorder, they could retrench twenty-five other staff members because people with an anxiety disorder do the work of five people without complaint! And we know this is so true!

For most people, anxiety disorders are stress-related, and our need to be all things to all people is an enormous and unnecessary stress. In seeking acceptance and approval from others, we suppress our own feelings, our needs and wants. If we add the day-to-day stress of living, and the major stresses that come our way, we can see that the development of our anxiety disorder is a natural response to all of the above.

Another way of looking at agoraphobia is to see it as a protection, not so much from panic attacks or anxiety symptoms but more of a protection from ourselves! If we are confined by the invisible boundaries of agoraphobia, we are limited in what we can do for others. Although agoraphobia can destroy our lives as we knew them to be, at the very least we can give ourselves a break from the demands we and other people place upon us.

As I noted in Chapter 7, intellectually we may understand that our symptoms are those of anxiety and panic. Intellectually, we may realise there is nothing physically wrong with us. Intellectually, we may know that our thoughts are creating our distress. But emotionally we do not feel the truth of this and emotionally we do not believe it.

Emotionally, we do not feel the truth of the countless positive statements and affirmations we repeat endlessly to ourselves, or the realistic statements we say to counteract negative thoughts.

Emotionally, we sabotage our intellectual understanding of our disorder and we become caught in the never-ending cycle of fear. In dealing with fear, we are dealing with emotions and no amount of intellectual dissection will integrate the two levels together without further understanding.

Recovery is a *change of perception*. We need to bring our emotional understanding of our disorder to the same level of our intellectual understanding. Emotionally, we need to learn to see and feel our panic attacks and anxiety for what they really are – panic and anxiety, nothing more. This does not negate the severity and strength of them. They can still feel as violent as before, but emotionally we can learn to see and feel why there is nothing to fear.

Learning to accept ourselves and learning to become responsible for ourselves is also part of this. *Learning* is the operative word. We can't go from non-acceptance to full acceptance in a minute. We need to learn about ourselves and how to become responsible for ourselves. The practice of mindfulness enables us to do this.

How did you feel when you read the last two paragraphs? Did you think, 'I don't know if I can do this.' 'This sounds all too hard.' 'I am too stupid for this.' 'I'll never be able to get it right.' 'What if I fail?'

With these and similar thoughts, we sabotage ourselves before we start. Yes, working towards recovery is hard work but we are not stupid and when we are being responsible for ourselves we won't fail – we will get it right!

Skilful compassionate action is the life raft, and self-responsibility and self-acceptance are the powers that can take us to full recovery and beyond. Not just to freedom from our disorder, but also to the freedom and security of being ourselves.

COMPASSION

Would you treat other people with an anxiety disorder in the same way as you are treating yourself? Take a moment to stop and think about this. Would you treat them with contempt? Dislike? Loathing? Hatred? Would you tell them they are stupid, weak, a failure or hopeless? Would you tell them they should just pull themselves together and get over it? Of course not. So why are you doing this to yourself? When other people are in pain, we do not abuse them, ignore them, run from them or hide from them. Yet this is exactly what we are doing to ourselves.

Many people with an anxiety disorder will say to me that all they want to do is to help other people who have an anxiety disorder. They say they do not want anyone else to experience the degree of suffering they have. Yet they don't recognise that they themselves are in need of the care and attention they so willingly want to give other people. We need to begin to care for ourselves the way we would care for another person with an anxiety disorder. We need to become our own 'rescuer'.

Compassion is the non-violation of self and the non-violation of others. In other words, causing no harm to yourself or to others. *No harm to yourself*. Many of us don't recognise how much we do harm ourselves. Our mental self-abuse and lack of kindness, care and respect towards ourselves causes a great deal of harm. Not only does it generate anxiety and depression, it compounds our already low self-esteem.

Compassion is skilful, active and powerful. This is not how we normally view compassion. In fact, compassion can be a difficult concept to fully understand, especially when we speak about becoming compassionate for ourselves. Many of us feel that this is being selfish, egocentric, or perhaps self-pitying. Compassion is none of these. It is our recognition of and active response to our pain and suffering.

A conversation I had with a client is a classic example of the way we think about ourselves:

CASE STUDY

A dialogue

Client: 'I know I have to like myself.'

Bronwyn: 'You have to like yourself? Whether you like it or not, you have to like yourself? What's the big flaw in your statement?'

Client: 'Have to.'

Bronwyn: 'Yes. *Have* to.'

Client: 'I suppose I should, anyway.'

Bronwyn: '*Should?*'

Client: 'Okay, okay. No shoulds. But you have read all the books. You know that we have to like ourselves or we have to love ourselves. I tried. I can't. It just makes everything worse.'

We have read all the books, stood in front of countless mirrors telling ourselves we are special, unique, that there is no one else like us in the universe and that we love ourselves. The problem with these thoughts is that we *do* feel we are special, we *do* feel we are unique and we *do* feel there is no one else in the universe like us, but we feel this in a disrespectful and disparaging way! Any feelings of love we try to conjure up are lost amongst the fragments of glass of the countless mirrors we have broken in anger and despair. Trying to like ourselves, to love ourselves because we have to, because we should, only increases the contempt we have for ourselves.

If we think we 'have to' care, like or love ourselves, then we are going to be in very big trouble! 'Having' to or 'should' means that these feelings are not coming naturally. 'I have to' and 'I should' tell us that this is another area where we think we have failed. The words trap us and give us no choice. We either 'have to' or we fail. There is no middle ground.

We can't manufacture feelings of liking or loving ourselves. They *arise naturally*, as a result of our caring enough about ourselves to treat ourselves with dignity and respect. Liking or loving ourselves is an effect of skilful compassionate action. When we can care for, accept and be responsible for ourselves, we appreciate and feel secure within ourselves because we are not betraying or invalidating ourselves.

How do you feel about you?

1. Do you love yourself?
2. Do you like yourself?
3. Do you dislike yourself?
4. Do you loathe yourself?
5. Do you hate yourself?
6. Do you feel apathetic towards yourself?
7. Have you never thought of it?

Do you recognise how points 1 and 2 impact on your mental health?

Do you recognise how points 3 and 7 impact on your mental health?

The first step in learning to care about ourselves is to become open to the idea that we are actually able to.

If you were speaking with another person with an anxiety

disorder, how would you advise them if they:

Thought their mental health was less important than other people's mental health?

Felt selfish in about caring about themselves?

Felt guilty in doing so?

Could not accept themselves as they are?

Felt that being responsible for themselves was egocentric or selfish?

How would you:

Comfort them?

Try to ease their pain and suffering?

How can you:

Comfort yourself?

Ease your own pain and suffering?

SELF-ACCEPTANCE

People say to me that they will accept themselves once they have recovered, once they have higher self-esteem. It doesn't work like this! Recovery and healthy self-esteem only happen once we have accepted ourselves as we are in this moment in time.

Learning to put ourselves first, and learning to work with the cause of our pain and suffering, is skilful compassionate action. It means we are beginning to accept ourselves, and that we are taking responsibility for ourselves. I know that some people struggle with self-acceptance because they think they have to accept that they are weak, stupid, hopeless and all the other abusive thoughts we can think about ourselves. But this is not the case. We are none of these things! These are *misperceptions* on our part. We will only realise this as we work through the process of recovery. There may be aspects of ourselves we want to change, and we can do this once we accept ourselves as we are right now.

Accepting ourselves right now, in this moment, means that we accept our strengths and perceived weaknesses. I say 'perceived' because we perceive that we are weak along with everything else! We are not weak, nor is having an anxiety disorder a sign of weakness. We have demanded and expected too much from ourselves for too long, and now we have been 'put on notice' to allow our emotional development to unfold.

When we can accept ourselves as we are, we accept the reality of ourselves and our circumstances as they are, not how we want them to be, how they should have to be or how they must be. We use so much energy trying to think away the reality of our experience and ourselves. 'If only. Once I recover. Once my self-esteem is higher. If this happens I can change. If that happens I can recover.'

We can wish and hope for change. But it is only when we accept ourselves in this current moment in time that we find we have a direction we can work towards. Instead of asking the question, 'Why am I like this?', we can find the answer to it.

The table below highlights the difference between non-acceptance and acceptance:

Non-acceptance	Self-acceptance
Unskilful action	Skilful action
Violation of self	Non-violation of self
Wanting everything to change	Being able to change
Drifting	Having a direction
Avoidance of our strengths	Acceptance of our strengths

Avoidance of our 'weakness'/ feelings of powerlessness	Acceptance of feelings of powerlessness and choosing to work to transform them
Feeling guilty about ourselves	Accepting ourselves as we are
Using energy in avoiding ourselves	Using our energy to change and develop
A continual sense of unease	A sense of initiative and intuition
Feelings of being out of control	Feelings of being in control
Being who we think we should be	Being ourselves

Accepting ourselves doesn't mean we accept that 'This is me and I am hopeless! This is my lot in life and I can't change.' It means 'This is me right now as I am in this moment. What can I do to help me become the person I want to be?'

Self-acceptance is something we need to consider. When we do, we can be open to the possibilities of who we can be and how our life can be. If we accept the challenge, it is a process of learning about and understanding ourselves. This is skilful action. The more we learn, the more exciting this becomes, because we begin to realise the potential of who we could be.

- What obstacles/blockages do you have in learning to accept yourself as you are?
- How can you overcome them?
- What fears do you have in learning to accept yourself?
- How can you overcome them?

ACCEPTING OUR DISORDER

In accepting ourselves as we are, we also accept that we have an anxiety disorder. There are two aspects of acceptance in this. The first is accepting that we have an anxiety disorder without feeling guilty about it, and without mentally abusing ourselves: 'I'm stupid, weak, hopeless.' This is not skilful or compassionate! These thoughts only generate further anxiety and depression.

When we develop our anxiety disorder it seems as if it is the 'proof' of how weak or stupid we are. This can be particularly so if we have spent years trying to fight our anxiety and panic to no avail. We don't recognise or acknowledge the fact that we may not have been diagnosed for years, and have not been taught any effective management skills. Yet we believe we should be able to 'pull ourselves together', even when our doctors haven't been able to diagnose exactly what it is we are experiencing! We are not weak or stupid, and part of our overall recovery is learning to accept the truth of this!

Secondly, some people think that if they accept that they have an anxiety disorder, they will have it for the rest of their lives. Other people don't like 'labels' and will reject a diagnosis of an anxiety disorder because of this. When we accept that we have an anxiety disorder, it doesn't mean we will have it for the rest of our lives. There is much more chance of this happening if we don't accept it! Once we accept it, we then have a starting point to begin the process of recovery. This also applies to 'labels'. If we reject the 'label' of an anxiety disorder, how do we recover? What is it we are trying to recover from?

Stages of acceptance

We are not cowards. Living with an anxiety disorder on a daily basis takes an enormous amount of strength and courage, and we need to recognise this and accept it.

Everyone says to me, 'I just want to recover.' My answer is, 'How much do you want to recover?' I say this for a reason, because of course we want to recover, but the full extent of our need and desire for recovery is hidden by our fears and symptoms. We have always been very passive people and we are very passive in our approach to our disorder. We all need to reach the point where we say 'enough is enough' and we begin to confront our fears, anxiety and panic head-on. This is a three-stage process.

First stage

The first stage is passive, and during this we all go through a period of complete non-acceptance and outright denial. This can range from a day or so to many months. No matter what we are told, no matter how many doctors we see, no matter how many clinical diagnostic tests we have, we simply don't believe that our symptoms and fears are those of an anxiety disorder.

We try to pull ourselves together, and we fight what is happening to us in the only way we know how. We resist it, we tense against it, we fight it mentally – 'I am not like this. How can this be happening to me?' – and the only thing that happens to us is that our anxiety and panic become stronger.

We are confused and frightened. It is during this stage that we can begin to develop agoraphobia. Ultimately, we exhaust ourselves in the fight and begin to accept that we have an anxiety disorder, which then generates even more fear. 'This is not me.' And while we accept our disorder at an intellectual level, we are caught up emotionally in the fear of our attacks and anxiety symptoms.

We feel trapped and wait impatiently for the next magic drug to be released or the next magic cure to come along. We wait for our doctor or therapist to set us free. But this doesn't happen and it won't happen. While they can support us, ultimately it is up to us to begin the process of working through to recovery. This is skilful action.

Second stage

Once we accept that we have an anxiety disorder, we move into the second stage, which is also passive. We may feel comfortable within a certain radius of our 'safe' places, home or work, but our fears still dominate. We may try to follow a cognitive behavioural program, but if we have an attack or become highly anxious, we can feel defeated and blame ourselves for our perceived 'failure'. And we still wish and hope for the magic drug or cure.

We can stay at this stage for some time, and then one of two things may happen. Our panic and anxiety can intensify, and we can feel ourselves slipping back to our original confused state of complete non-acceptance. Or we can become angry and frustrated at our limitations, at the nagging anxiety and constant fear of having another attack. 'Enough is enough!' Our anger and frustration become stronger than our fears, panic and anxiety, and we move into the third and final stage of acceptance. We are no longer passive in our approach to our disorder. We become proactive. This is also skilful action.

Third stage

We feel the need to recover in every cell of our being, and we know that nothing is going to stand in our way. Our attitude becomes,

'No matter what the cost, I am going to recover' – and I don't mean financial cost! 'No matter what the cost' means that we become disciplined in our approach to recovery. We make time to meditate, or use another relaxation technique. We become disciplined in using a mindfulness cognitive technique or other cognitive techniques, and we work on our avoidance behaviours. We practise every day, and although we are still overcome by our fears and symptoms, we pick ourselves up and we take them head-on again and again. And ultimately we win as a result of these skilful actions.

SELF-RESPONSIBILITY

Accepting our disorder and ourselves, and understanding why we have developed our disorder, is compassionate and skilful. It is also the first of a series of steps we take in becoming responsible for ourselves and our recovery.

We all want to recover, yet some people will hesitate, delay or refuse to begin to take the necessary steps to enable them to recover. One of the first reasons we delay is 'time'. We simply don't have the time to work on our recovery, despite the fact that our disorder may be taking up all the time we have each day!

When I first began to teach people to meditate I would say to them, 'Meditate twice a day for twenty minutes.' They would look at me and say, 'Are you kidding? I have to do this, I have to do that. And I must do this and should do that.' So I would say, 'Okay, meditate once a day for twenty minutes.' They would look at me again and say, 'Are you kidding. I have to do this and I have to do that and . . .'

Usually, everything we have to do, must do, should do is for everyone else! Our recovery needs to be our number one priority, but in most instances we don't treat our recovery as a priority. It may be number five, ten or twenty on our list of things to do.

When I ask people with an anxiety disorder what it is they need the most, everyone looks at me questioningly. They are not able to give me a definitive answer. When I ask them about their need to recover, they hesitate for a moment and then acknowledge, 'Yes, of course.' Initially, they don't see their recovery in the context of a personal need. They are too busy taking care of the needs of everyone else to realise that they have needs of their own.

If we are committed to recovery we are going to need to make time for it! This means learning to say no to other people – and as we all know, the word 'no' is not in our vocabulary. Yet this is what we are going to need to do, especially in the early stages of the recovery process. Our mental health demands nothing less. This is skilful action.

Learning to say no can be very frightening, especially when we are putting our own needs before others. We feel it is one of the worst things in life that we can do. We feel guilty; we feel selfish; we feel we are being bad, uncaring, unsympathetic and everything else in between, even just thinking about saying no.

We need to begin to question our beliefs that tell us our needs are not important or are irrelevant, and that our mental health is less important than other people's. Taking time for ourselves to work on our recovery is being responsible for ourselves. It is not being selfish, nor does it have anything to do with selfishness. Working towards our own health is healthy! Not taking the time we need is abdicating our responsibility to ourselves. If other people argue the point and accuse us of being selfish, then we need to ask ourselves, 'Who is it that is being selfish?' While there may be some short-term difficulties in learning to say no, they are far outweighed by the long-term benefits to ourselves and our family.

The bottom line is that our motivation and our priority needs to be for ourselves and our recovery. And making time to work on our recovery each day is being responsible for ourselves.

In one of my workshops, I asked participants what self-responsibility meant to them during the recovery process. Their answers are listed below:

What self-responsibility means

- Making our recovery our number one priority
- Recognising that our mental health is just as important as our physical health
- Recognising that no one's mental health is more important than our own
- Working in partnership with ourselves, not in opposition to ourselves
- Treating ourselves with dignity and respect
- Making a commitment to ourselves to work through to recovery
- Taking responsibility for our own recovery from this moment on
- Taking responsibility for doing whatever we need to do for ourselves
- Recognising and accepting that working towards recovery is not selfish, it is healthy
- Acknowledging and accepting the fact that we have an anxiety disorder, and that our doctor would not have made the diagnosis if they were not sure. If we doubt it, then it is our responsibility to seek a second opinion. Once the diagnosis is confirmed, we need to accept it.
- Being totally honest with our doctor about what we are experiencing, including any suicidal thoughts. Our doctor can't make a full assessment of our situation if we are not being completely honest with them.

- If our doctor doesn't have the current knowledge of anxiety disorders then it is our responsibility to find a doctor who does
- Recognising that asking for and accepting help is healthy – there is no reason to feel guilty or bad about doing so
- Becoming informed about any medication we are taking
- Seeing that there is a choice in everything we think and do
- Not blaming ourselves for having an anxiety disorder
- Accepting the fact that we are *not* weak, stupid or hopeless
- Stopping the mental self-abuse
- Learning all we can about our anxiety disorder
- Understanding our symptoms and why they are happening
- Becoming disciplined in practising meditation or another relaxation technique, as well as becoming disciplined in a cognitive technique

Part 3

Managing panic attacks and anxiety

CHAPTER 9

Meditation

Meditation has been the subject of research since the late 1960s, and it is now being used in many treatments in conjunction with conventional medicine. Meditation also reduces anxiety levels in anxiety disorders. One study showed 'significant reductions in anxiety and depression' and demonstrated its effectiveness in panic disorder with or without agoraphobia, and generalised anxiety disorder (Kabat-Zinn et al, 1992).

All we need to start the recovery process is an openness to learn, and the determination to recover. Of course, we all want to recover right now, at this moment, but we know this is not going to happen. And so we start the process of recovery by accepting that it is going to take time and that we need to learn patience – patience with ourselves and patience with the recovery process. We can't learn and develop our skills in a day or so.

When we learn to drive, we aren't able to get into a car and drive straight onto the Formula 1 circuit. We need to learn how to drive first, and with ongoing practice we become more relaxed and skilful in our driving. As our skills develop, we learn how to drive under different conditions and on different terrain. It is the same process in whatever we do. We don't start university and receive a PhD the next day. We don't learn to ski and be immediately accepted into the Olympic team. We need to learn and develop our skills.

So too with our recovery. Recovery is a learning process and we need to approach it in this way. We need to learn about our panic and anxiety. The more we learn about them, the more power we are going to have to help us manage them permanently, but this is going to take time, effort and energy. We can't just read about meditation, mindfulness or other cognitive techniques, try them once or twice and then wonder why they aren't working. We need to put them into practice. We need to become disciplined in our approach to recovery in the same way that 'would be' Formula 1 drivers, PhD students or 'would be' Olympic skiers do.

WHY MEDITATION?

I teach people to meditate for two main reasons. First, because it is a relaxation technique; and second, because meditation is the oldest cognitive technique in the world. Its simplicity and gracefulness have stood the test of time.

The cognitive aspect of meditation is different from other cognitive therapies. The major difference is the practice of mindfulness (awareness), which is the fundamental principle of mindfulness meditation. Mindfulness teaches us to detach ourselves from the thinking process. It separates thinker from thought. Mindfulness teaches us to observe and watch the play of the mind, to see how we move from one thought to another, from one mind state to another. As we observe this process, we learn to see very clearly that we have a choice in what we think about.

In other cognitive therapies, there is no separation between thinker and thought. These therapies use various thinking techniques such as realistic thinking, in which we examine our anxiety and panic thoughts and replace them with more objective thoughts. We remain attached to the thinking process and use thought to 'defeat' thought.

Meditation also differs from progressive muscle relaxation techniques. These techniques focus on relaxing our body, muscle group by muscle group. From my experience, these techniques work for some people, but many people experience difficulty with them. One of the main problems with these techniques is that they focus on the body. They don't take into account the fact that many of us are already doing this. We are very much focused on the body! We are constantly checking for symptoms and monitoring them, and we are continually tensing up, ready for action should we have even a hint of one.

When we begin using a progressive muscle relaxation technique, we can be going through the motions of tensing and un-tensing but our mind is still on auto pilot, scanning to see what the symptoms are doing or not doing, and scanning to see how we are feeling. 'Am I relaxed yet? Why aren't I relaxed?' Or we can be tensing our already tense muscles, and then releasing the tension back to our original tenseness. 'Gosh that feels better – I don't think so!'

Meditation works in the opposite way. Meditation relaxes our mind and our body relaxes in response to this. Meditation also teaches us to become aware of our automatic thoughts, and our monitoring and checking of symptoms. It teaches us to see that we actually do have a choice in what we think about, and teaches us to control our thoughts, including 'Am I relaxed yet? Why aren't I relaxed?'

In this chapter we will look at meditation in a number of ways:
- As a relaxation technique
- To learn mindfulness (awareness) skills
- To learn how not to attach to or empower our thoughts
- As an exposure technique for dissociative states, including depersonalisation and derealisation
- As an exposure technique for letting go of the need to be in control

In the following chapters we will learn how to apply mindfulness skills in everyday life so that we can become:
- Mindful of our panic- and anxiety-producing thoughts
- Aware of the intimate relationship between our thoughts and our symptoms
- Aware of any tendency to dissociate

This will assist us to:
- See how many of our fears and symptoms are being created by the way we think
- See that we have a choice in what we think about
- Learn not to attach to or empower our thoughts
- Learn how to manage and control our thoughts
- Learn to let go of the need to fight our panic attacks and anxiety
- Learn to let our panic attacks and anxiety happen without resistance
- Be aware of and manage any personal tendency to dissociate

After reading this list, you may be wondering how all of this can be achieved through meditation. But it can if you are motivated

and prepared to become disciplined in the practice of meditation
and mindfulness as a cognitive technique.

WHEN AND WHERE?

When I am teaching people to meditate I break every rule in the
book. The aim of this meditation is recovery, not Nirvana. Well,
perhaps the 'Nirvana' of recovery, but as we are not using meditation for spiritual purposes, we can allow ourselves to be more
flexible. This flexibility enables people to meditate without needing to go through a check list of 'shoulds' and 'should nots' – how
to sit, where to sit, when to sit and when not to sit. A list of
'shoulds and should nots' only creates further worry and anxiety,
and meditation just becomes one more thing we have to do. And
do perfectly.

The first rule I break is 'when to meditate'. We can meditate
any time during the day or early evening, as long as we commit
to meditating at least once a day. All we need is twenty minutes.
This can be on the bus or train on our way to or from work, during a lunch break or we can wake twenty minutes earlier in the
morning and use this time while family members are still asleep.

We may be able to meditate sometime in the afternoon one day,
and find we can schedule a meditation session the following day
in the evening. As long as we make a commitment and become
disciplined in setting time aside, even if it is only one twenty-
minute session a day, we will feel the benefits. And this is all that
matters.

The second rule I break is 'do not lie down'. If you feel more
comfortable lying down, then do so. Lying down makes it easier
to go to sleep, but the third rule I break is 'do not go to sleep'.
Many people are exhausted through their disorder. As they begin

to relax, whether they are sitting or lying down, they may drift off to sleep in the first few weeks of practice. If they do go to sleep during meditation, it means they need it! People will stay awake once they are not so exhausted. It also means they have let go of their need to be in control at all times. Learning to let go of this control is one of the most important aspects in recovery.

One 'rule' I do set is don't meditate just before going to sleep at night. As we become more comfortable with meditation, we will find that we can feel revitalised after a session and may not feel like going to sleep. To avoid this happening, schedule any evening meditation session two or three hours before going to bed.

In contradiction to this, however, many people have difficulties going to sleep at night as a result of their anxiety. If this is the case we can use our meditation technique to put ourselves to sleep at night. When we are ready to go to sleep we can begin to meditate and allow ourselves to let go, and our meditation will take us gently and easily into sleep. In short we can meditate anytime of the day as long as we commit to meditating at least once a day.

DO NOT DISTURB!

A number of people say to me that family members don't take them seriously when they ask not to be disturbed while they meditate. Our need for privacy and quiet time needs to be respected, as our recovery is most important. Not only will we benefit, so will our family as we begin to recover. Respect your needs, take them seriously, and your family will learn to accept them.

Divert the phone. If there is one thing we can be sure of it's that the phone will not ring all day, but the minute we sit for meditation the 'whole world' will be ringing us!

Put pets outside. Nothing destroys a meditation session so

completely as a cat or dog jumping onto our lap while we are deep in meditation.

Time the meditation session. We can meditate either with or without music. If we prefer to use music, we can choose a piece of music that will last for twenty minutes. If we decide to meditate without music, we can use a watch or non-ticking clock to time our session. During our meditation we can gently open our eyes and check the time. If the twenty minutes is not over, we simply return to our meditation. Within a few days we will know when the twenty minutes are over without needing to open our eyes. Don't use an alarm clock or any other timer. Meditation is for relaxing, and we won't be feeling very relaxed if we are brought out of meditation by the ringing or beeping of a clock or timer.

When our meditation is over, sit quietly for a few minutes. This allows us to come out of meditation gently and quietly.

MEDITATION AS A RELEASE

When people first learn to meditate, I suggest they only meditate for twenty minutes at a time. Meditation is a 'releasing process'. On occasion we could experience feelings that we have been suppressing, such as our anger or sadness. This is similar to the 'releasing process' that can occur when some people have a massage. They find they feel sad or angry during the massage, or immediately afterwards. The releasing process doesn't usually begin within the twenty-minute period of meditation. Even if it does, the release of these feelings is healthy. When we keep the feelings suppressed, they can add extra fuel to our anxiety disorder.

This is the reason I suggest people stay within the twenty-minute time frame. As we become more familiar and comfortable with the process of meditation, we can extend our meditation time if we want to – and many people do!

THE MINDFULNESS OF MEDITATION

One of the most common problems people have when they first learn to meditate is that they try to think of 'nothing' or to 'blank' their mind. This is a contradiction. The more we try to think of 'nothing', the more thoughts we will have, because these are also just thoughts. 'I have to think of nothing, why can't I think of nothing, why can't I blank my mind out, blank out, blank out, why can't I do this?'

Meditation is not a process of trying to *eliminate* all thoughts and feelings. Rather, it is a process of 'letting go' of our attachment to our thoughts and feelings. When we can let go of our thoughts, the profound quiet of meditation unfolds gently and naturally.

'Letting go of our attachment.' What did you think when you read the word 'attachment'? Did you think, 'What is she talking about?' Did you analyse the word 'attachment', trying to work out exactly what I meant? If so, you became attached to the thought about 'attachment'. You were thinking about what the word meant in this context. And we do become 'attached' to our thoughts every waking moment. A thought rises into consciousness, we attach to it and we attach to the next thought and the next and so on.

How did you feel when you were trying to work out what I meant by the word 'attachment?' Did you feel confused? Slightly annoyed? What many of us don't realise is that *our thoughts create our feeling states*, including our fears, anxiety, panic, confusion and annoyance.

Meditation is a process of observing our thoughts, rather than attaching to them. We become mindful; that is, we become aware of our thoughts as they rise into consciousness. We see how we attach to our thoughts, and become involved with our thinking. In meditation, we let go of our thinking and the thought falls away; another thought will rise and if we don't attach to it, it will fall away. As our meditation deepens, our thoughts slow down and disappear by themselves, as we enter the full meditative state. And in this state there are no thoughts or feelings, only an all-encompassing silence and peace.

MEDITATION TECHNIQUES

I am going to describe three different meditation techniques that I teach in my workshops. One is a 'word' technique, the second a 'breathing' technique and the third an 'image' technique. These techniques give us an object to focus our mind on. It isn't a matter of analysing the word or becoming involved in the breathing process or creating an elaborate image. They are simply objects that we use to detach from our thoughts.

Our thoughts have always had control over us. Meditation teaches us how to control them. One of my meditation teachers used the analogy that meditation trains our minds in a similar way to how we train a puppy to 'sit' on command. We say, 'Sit,' and the puppy looks at us, 'Yes, sure,' and runs away. We bring the puppy back and say, 'Sit,' and it runs away. We bring the puppy back, 'Sit,' and away it runs again. In time the puppy learns to 'sit' and in time so will our minds!

We 'sit' our mind on the word or breath or image, and immediately our mind runs away with a thought. We become aware, let the thought go, and bring our mind back and 'sit' it on the word or breath or image, and it runs away again.

This is the process of meditation. Our thoughts are part of this process. Many people think that they should not be thinking, and they become frustrated when their thoughts constantly break through their meditation. Becoming frustrated means we are attaching to our thoughts about our thoughts!

Word technique

This technique involves the silent repetition of a word or a mantra. The word or mantra becomes the object of our meditation – a point to focus our mind on.

While we can use any word we like, it is preferable to use a short word with one or two syllables. In his book *'The Relaxation Response'*, Herbert Benson suggests the word 'one' (Benson, 1995). I always advise people not to use words like 'peace' or 'calm' as these words can have negative associations, such as 'Calm down!' or 'Why can't I get any peace?' This is not very conducive to meditation. Some people use a word that has meaning for them, perhaps a word from the Bible. Other people use everyday words such as 'rose'.

Some people prefer a mantra. 'Om', pronounced 'aum', is a well-known mantra. 'Shantih' is another, which has been translated as meaning 'peace'; another mantra is 'sharma', interpreted as meaning 'quietude'.

Breathing technique

The object of this technique is to focus on our breath. Some people have fears and anxiety associated with their breathing. I advise people who have these particular fears to use a word or image technique instead.

There are two variations with the breathing technique, and both follow the natural rhythm of the breath. There is no need to alter our breathing in any way.

The first technique is to become mindful of the sensation of our breath, as we inhale and exhale. Being aware of the sensations of each breath becomes the object of our meditation.

A variation of this is to count each breath. The first breath we take when we sit for meditation becomes breath number one. The next is breath number two, and so on until breath number five. After this breath we begin the count again at one, and so on.

Image technique

Some people are more 'visual' and prefer to visualise an image as their object of meditation. It is important that we only use this technique if we are a 'visual' person, otherwise we will have difficulty trying to visualise and will become frustrated and annoyed, the opposite to what we could be feeling.

If we decide to use this technique, I always advise people to keep the image simple. Some people may visualise a flower or a bird in flight. If we construct a more elaborate visualisation we may spend the whole twenty minutes trying to get it perfect! The more complicated the image we use, the more it keeps us attached to our thoughts.

PRACTICE OF MEDITATION

The encompassing framework of this meditation is mindfulness – being aware. Depending on our individual choice, when we sit for meditation we will:

- silently repeat a word or mantra to ourselves, or

- become aware of the sensations of our breath as we inhale and exhale, or
- focus on the image we have chosen to visualise.

As we do this, our thoughts will break through almost immediately, and we will attach to our thoughts and become involved with them. We need to become aware that we are thinking and not focusing on our object of meditation. We become mindful; that is, we become aware, we observe, we witness, that we are thinking. We let the thought go, and bring our mind back to the word, breath or image. Another thought will rise, and we will attach to this one. We become aware that we are thinking, we let go of the thought, and bring our mind back to the object of our meditation.

When we sit for meditation we:

- Focus on the word or breath or image we have chosen
- Lose the focus by becoming attached to our thoughts
- Become aware we are thinking, not meditating
- Let go of our thoughts, stop thinking on them
- Bring our focus back to the object of our meditation
- Become caught up in our thinking again
- Become aware we are thinking, not meditating
- Let go of our thoughts
- Bring our focus back to the object
- And we will become attached to our thoughts
- And we let go of our thoughts and we . . .

This is the process of meditation. Some people become annoyed or frustrated as their thoughts break through time and again. If we are becoming frustrated, be aware that this is also just a thought. Let the thought go, and come back to the word or breath or image.

BECOMING RELAXED

One of the most common problems people have when they are learning to meditate is that they try to relax. We become relaxed when we don't try. As our meditation progresses, we will begin to relax without effort. As we do so, our thoughts will slow down by themselves.

If we are using a word or mantra, we will become aware that our normal inner 'speaking' voice has also slowed down. The repetition of the word or mantra will be slow and possibly drawn out. Let this happen. If we bring our inner repetition back to our normal rhythm, we will bring ourselves out of meditation.

Irrespective of what object we are using in our meditation, our breathing will slow down naturally and easily by itself. Allow the breath to slow down. If we bring the breath back to its normal rhythm, we will bring ourselves out of meditation.

This also applies to the image we may be visualising. We will lose the clarity of the image. Allow this to happen. If we bring it back into clarity, we will come out of meditation. These are the signs that we are becoming relaxed.

Let whatever happens, happen. If you feel anxious, allow yourself to feel anxious; if you feel bored, allow yourself to feel bored; if you feel frustrated, allow yourself to feel frustrated; if you are beginning to feel relaxed, allow yourself to feel relaxed. In all instances, let the thoughts go and bring your mind back onto the object of meditation. We may reach the point where the object of our meditation and our thoughts disappear completely, leaving us in the all-encompassing awareness of the silence of our mind.

At the end of the twenty minutes, give yourself some time to return to your normal waking state. Sit quietly for a few minutes and open your eyes when you feel comfortable.

CASE HISTORIES

Mira

It was Mira's first meditation lesson. She was feeling apprehensive. She glanced around the room and wondered if other people were feeling the same way. She closed her eyes and began to practise the meditation technique she had chosen. At first she felt self-conscious and she couldn't understand how this would help her with her anxiety and panic attacks. Gradually, she became aware of a gentle heaviness slowly moving through her body. A wave of fear swept through her, but she allowed it to pass without resisting it. She felt herself drifting into deeper and deeper levels of relaxation. The voice of Mira's instructor, ending the meditation session, broke into the silent depths of her meditation. Slowly Mira opened her eyes. She had done it. She was able to meditate.

Stephan

Finding the time to meditate was a problem for Stephan. He had been practising meditation on and off for several months, and had become aware that he always had a bad day if he didn't meditate the night before. He wished there was an easier way to control his anxiety. He 'didn't have time' and it was such an effort to try to make time to meditate. He felt he would just have to put up with the anxiety until a 'real cure' was found.

Vashti

'I did it! I did it!' Vashti told her husband. 'I was so scared when we started. Then I felt myself relaxing, and that scared me. It has been so long since I have relaxed. I got confused and that made me anxious. But I just let it happen and kept my mind focused on the word and then I realised it was just the tension draining away. And I felt great. Then I had an attack. I couldn't believe it. I was so relaxed. But I kept on going. I let that happen as well. And it disappeared so fast. It just shot through me and it was gone. I just kept on focusing on my word and I went deeper into meditation. Then suddenly the time was up. I didn't want it to end. I felt so fantastic.'

Meditation is so hard to do, because it is so simple! Don't complicate it by thinking:

- Am I doing it right?
- How do I know it is right?
- It has to work, if not I won't recover
- How is this going to help?
- I don't get the point of all of this
- I feel a bit silly doing this
- Is it happening yet?
- I don't really have time to do this
- Why can't I just relax and watch TV?
- What is this supposed to feel like?
- This isn't working, I'll try the breath
- What's for lunch?
- That doesn't work
- I'm bored
- What about a mantra?
- I should try the word again
- What does a mantra really mean?
- Do I really want to use a mantra?
- Is it happening yet?

- I will use another word – 'rose'
- I can't do this, I'm useless
- Why isn't it happening?
- What's for dinner?
- How do I do this and plan my day?
- Maybe I should use the word and breath
- Everyone else can do this but me
- Am I focusing on both the word and breath?
- How do I do that?
- Is it happening yet?
- Is it twenty minutes yet?
- What am I supposed to feel like?
- What am I going to do after this?
- Fifteen minutes to go!
- I should try it some other time
- This isn't working
- I can't see how this will work
- Perhaps it will work tomorrow
- I'll try again then

These are just thoughts. Detach from them, let them go and bring your mind back to the object of your meditation.

CHAPTER 10

Meditation – questions and answers

IF MEDITATION IS SO SIMPLE, WHY IS IT SO HARD?

People have many questions when they first begin to meditate. The following is a list of every question I have ever been asked about meditation. Use this list to help you understand any difficulties you may have in regards to your meditation practice. Check the boxes of the points you may be having difficulty with and work your way through them, one by one if you need to, during your meditation session.

Basic meditation practice

☐ Do I have to use music?
Some people prefer to use music, others don't. It is an individual choice.

☐ I feel very self-conscious when I start to meditate
People can feel self-conscious when they first begin. Be mindful that this is also just thought. Let it go and bring your mind back to the object of your meditation.

☐ I can't make up my mind whether to use a word or breath or
   an image

Some people do become confused. They can spend many sessions trying one or the other, or all three, wondering why they can't meditate. We need to choose one and give ourselves time to become familiar with it. Listen to your intuition. Which one feels more comfortable, more right for you?

☐ I am not sure about awareness. How do I do that?

Awareness, mindfulness, is 'stepping back' and watching the passing parade of your thoughts. Instead of attaching to your thoughts, being caught up in them, you detach from them and simply observe them.

☐ I am not sure about letting the thoughts go

It is a matter of letting them come into your mind and not attaching to them. As you become aware that you are thinking, you can choose not to think about them. Let the thoughts go, stop thinking and bring your mind back to the object of your meditation. In much the same way as police direct traffic, we become our own 'thought' police. We can either allow a thought to 'go through', or we can mentally hold our hand in the stop position and 'wave' our attention back onto the object of our meditation.

☐ I seem to have both object and thoughts at the same time

This can be the case for some people. You focus on the word or breath or image, and there is a 'background' of thoughts running through your mind. You attach to your thoughts and they come into the 'foreground' while the object of meditation moves into the background. When you become aware that your primary focus is on your thoughts, let them go and return your focus back to the object. This will bring the object back to the foreground and your thoughts will move to the background.

☐ I don't like seeing my thoughts
This is only a thought! But yes, some people are frightened of seeing their thoughts. They think to themselves, 'I don't want to know!' and they will avoid meditation and mindfulness. The problem is although we may avoid seeing them, that doesn't mean they disappear! They are still there and they are creating our anxiety and panic, which none of us like at all! To recover, we need to understand our disorder intimately. We need to see the 'nuts and bolts' of it so we can dismantle it.

When you practise mindfulness meditation you are separating yourself from your thoughts. You may not like them, you may be frightened of them at first, but see them for what they are. Thoughts. That's all. They are not the sum total of you. If they were, you would not be able to learn how to control them by letting them go. And you can control them. Just note the thought, 'I don't like seeing my thoughts', and let it go. If you are feeling anxious about them, make a mental note, 'feeling anxious', let go of the thought and let the anxiety be there. Experiment with your thoughts. Investigate your thoughts. Become aware of how they are creating what you are feeling. When you can see this emotionally, you will then know why there is nothing to fear.

☐ I am scared of how my body feels when I am meditating
Many people who have not been able to relax for so long can become frightened of the sensations of their body relaxing. Don't attach to the fearful thoughts. Just note, 'body relaxing', and let the thought go. Let your body feel whatever it is feeling. Just let it happen. The unknown of meditation becomes the known with practice!

☐ I can't stop thinking
☐ I can't blank my mind
☐ I can't think of nothing

Don't even try! Trying to stop thinking, trying to blank your mind, trying to think of nothing – these are simply thoughts. Let them go and come back to the object of your meditation. Your thoughts will slow down or disappear completely as you move into the deeper stages of meditation.

☐ My eyes keep wanting to partially open

Let this happen. Don't fight it. Go with whatever happens.

☐ I am not sure if I am meditating
☐ Why isn't my meditation happening?
☐ I don't know if I am doing it right

If you are looking for meditation to happen, then it is almost guaranteed not to! Don't check for signs that you are actually meditating. Let go of your thoughts about it. Meditation happens when we least expect it to.

If you realise your breathing has slowed down, or if the meditation session went quickly, or if you experienced one or some of the effects listed below, then you were meditating.

☐ My thoughts race out of control

Simply note the thought, 'my thoughts are racing', and bring your mind back to the word or breath or image. Your thoughts will slow down once you stop giving them the attention.

☐ I am worried about my breathing slowing down

The slowing down in breathing is a sign your meditation is going well. Note the thought, 'worried about my breathing', and let it go, and come back to the focus of your meditation. Don't attach to the thought, let it fall away. Let whatever happens, happen. Go with the flow of your meditation. If you need to take a deep breath or your breathing needs to return to its normal rate, it will do so automatically.

☐ I get bored

Note the thought, 'bored', let it go and return to the object of your meditation. Are you sure that your boredom is not part of a need to be in control. A defence against letting go of control? See 'Need to be in control' below.

☐ I get distracted by outside noises

This happens to everyone. I remember once teaching a large group of people to meditate during a winter storm. As we began, a huge thunderstorm moved overhead. The lightning was flashing and the thunder was extremely loud. The wind increased. Then it began to rain and hail very heavily. I thought to myself, no one is going to be able to meditate in this. Yet, almost all the group did. They simply noted the noise of the storm, and returned their attention back to the object of their meditation.

Simply note your thoughts about being distracted, let them go and come back to the word or breath or image.

☐ All of my meditations are different

And they will be. Some will be great, others won't. Take it as it comes. Each meditation session will teach you more about the overall process, even the ones you think are not so good.

☐ My meditation goes so fast

You are meditating well! This is what happens when you do.

☐ My meditation goes too slowly

Are you becoming attached to thoughts like 'When is the time up?' or 'How much longer do I have to do this?' Simply note the thoughts, let them go and come back to the focus of your meditation. But be mindful that this may be a defence against letting go of control. See below.

☐ I come out of meditation too easily

This may be happening for a couple of reasons. As your breath slows, you may be bringing your breath back to its normal rhythm. Equally, as the repetition of the word or mantra slows down, you may be bringing it back to the normal rhythm of your inner speaking voice. If you are using an image and it becomes distorted during meditation, you may be bringing the image back to full clarity. Any of these occurrences will bring you out of meditation very quickly. Go with the slowing down of the breath and/or the word or mantra or any distortions of the image. Let it happen.

Or you may be 'on guard', waiting and watching for something to happen – and I don't mean waiting for your meditation to happen! You may have your radar turned on checking for symptoms, or you may be having difficulty in letting go of control. See below.

Sometimes we may come out of meditation spontaneously, and feel quite refreshed. If this happens, finish your meditation session and don't attach to your thoughts about why this happened. This is just part of the overall experience of meditation.

☐ I am frightened I will not be able to come out of meditation

This doesn't happen. Breaking our meditation is easy. See the above question.

☐ I can't seem to make the time to meditate or practise any form of relaxation

This can be avoidance, rather than not finding the time. Is it perhaps a fear of letting go of control? Or is it because you feel safe within your comfort zone, and feel frightened of doing something new? If so, what can you do to assist yourself in working through this?

Do you perhaps feel annoyed or frustrated that you 'have' to do something? Many of us think, 'Why do I have to do this?' We can feel resentful and this can hold us back in working towards recovery. We need to see that we are hurting ourselves by not making time to work on our recovery.

☐ I only feel relaxed in meditation – I don't feel relaxed during the day

This is normal when we first begin to meditate. Keep practising and you will find the benefits will gradually extend into everyday life. Perhaps for only a few minutes in the beginning, but with continued practice you will feel it extending further.

The need to be in control

☐ I want to meditate but can't
☐ I am too frightened to meditate
☐ I can't let go of control
☐ I can't meditate alone
☐ I feel very anxious before and when I meditate
☐ I feel very tense as I start to meditate
☐ I can't sit still
☐ I feel frightened after my meditations

All these observations reflect one need – the need to be in control. We have always needed to be in control of ourselves and of our environment. This need to be in control is the 'super glue' that holds in place the many different masks we wear that enable us to be 'all things to all people'.

The only thing we are not in control of is our thinking. Recovery means that we need to let go of our need to be in control, and learn to control our thinking instead. Some people can be very frightened of letting go of the control, because they fear their worst fears will come true. They don't. The need to be in control is helping to perpetuate our disorder. We will only recover once we can let go of this need to be in control. When we do, the only thing that will happen to us is we will recover!

It is all right to feel anxious, tense and nervous when we begin to meditate. We are learning a new skill, and this new skill is going to take us out of our 'comfort zone'. We need to allow ourselves to feel anxious, to feel tense and to feel frightened. We can 'hold' hands with our fears and anxiety, and begin to meditate. Simply let the feelings be there, and don't become attached to the thoughts about them. Let them happen and gently bring your mind back to the object of meditation.

If it becomes too uncomfortable, we need to be able to note the thought, 'very uncomfortable', and bring our mind back to the object of our meditation. If we attach to our thoughts about how frightened or anxious we may feel, we will only increase these feelings. Let them happen and don't attach to thoughts about them.

If we find we are not able to do this, finish the meditation session. Not with thoughts of failure or 'I will never be able to do this', but with thought, 'I will see how I go tomorrow.'

Even if it means sitting for meditation for only five minutes, this is a starting point. The next day we can see if we can increase this time to six minutes. The following day to seven minutes, and so on. The most important point is to practise letting go to the point where we feel comfortable, and then seeing if we can slowly increase it, minute by minute.

Letting go of the need to be in control when we sit for meditation is exactly the same as when we go to sleep at night. Most people don't think about letting go of control when they go to sleep. They simply do it. And nothing happens to them except they go to sleep! The same applies with our meditation practice. Nothing happens to us. We simply meditate.

We may be able to meditate and let go of the control without even thinking about it. When we have finished meditating, we may realise that we were indeed meditating and we have actually let go of the control. Some people can become frightened of this, but this too is just a thought. The fact that nothing happened to them during their meditation demonstrates very clearly that the only thing that happens is that we relax. Instead of attaching to the fearful thoughts, we need to attach to the fact that nothing happened to us and nothing will happen to us when we let go of this control.

The effects of meditation

- ☐ I see colours swirling when I meditate
- ☐ I feel very light
- ☐ I feel very heavy
- ☐ My thoughts seem to disappear and it is as if I am watching a movie
- ☐ I can see images when I meditate
- ☐ I feel as if I am floating
- ☐ I am losing awareness of my body or parts of my body

☐ I see a white light or flashes of white light or thousands of pinpricks of white light

Quite a number of people who dissociate will experience some of these sensations in meditation and also sometimes as they are going to sleep at night. People who don't dissociate can also experience these when they meditate.

As I said above, meditation can become an exposure technique for people who do dissociate. During meditation we can become aware of how easy it is to move in and out of different states of consciousness. We can also realise how peaceful these states can be when we don't fear them.

These sensations are also signs that we are relaxing deeply and that our meditation is going well. Let go of any thoughts associated with them and let them happen. Enjoy!

☐ I can't get used to the sensations. I don't like them
If we find we are becoming frightened of these sensations, all we need do is note the thought and return our mind to the object of meditation. Don't attach to your thoughts about them, including the thought 'I don't like them!' Just be aware of the sensations, let them happen and bring your mind back to your object of focus. They will disappear. You may find that you can enjoy these sensations once you let go of any fearful or 'judging' thoughts about them.

☐ I never get these sensations
Some people will have one or more of these sensations; others will never experience any of them. It doesn't matter if these sensations don't occur. It doesn't mean we are not meditating; it means they don't happen. They are simply effects some people can have when they meditate.

Don't spend your meditation sessions watching and waiting for any of these sensations to happen. This is guaranteed to ensure they won't!

☐ I had an attack-like sensation in meditation

This can happen occasionally. If it does happen, we can use it to enormous advantage. This is how I learnt to recover. I would sometimes experience an attack in meditation, and instead of attaching to my thoughts of 'Oh no', I would simply bring my mind back to the object of my meditation. I realised that by doing so, the attack would move through and disappear as fast as it had come. This is one of the big secrets of recovery. When we allow ourselves to let the attack happen, it shows us how fast it can disappear, and also shows us why there is nothing to fear.

☐ I am aware of when I reach the thought-free state, and then
  I think to myself 'I have reached the thought free state' and it
  disappears. How can I stay in this state longer?

Don't think to yourself 'I have reached the thought-free state' or thoughts to that effect! When any thoughts break through this state, just be aware and gently let them go, and quietly come back to the word or breath or image. This is the process of meditation.

☐ Yes, no, maybe?

After teaching people to meditate, I ask them if they felt their meditation session was beneficial. I also ask what difficulties they may have experienced. It's interesting to note that some people who indicate that they had difficulties with their meditation, actually didn't! In speaking with them, I find that they may have been anxious as they began to meditate. Or they may initially have had difficulty in letting go of their thoughts, or the need to be in control. Yet overall they felt very relaxed, their breathing had slowed down and the session time had gone quickly.

They were discounting the fact that they were able to meditate successfully. Their mind picked up on the initial difficulties they experienced, and they attached to their thoughts that the session didn't go well.

Meditation is only hard because we make it so by thinking about it. If you read through my responses to the questions, you will see the central theme of meditation: become aware, let go of the thought and let it happen.

Simplicity itself!

CHAPTER 11

Mind states

PERCEPTION

Imagine you have been out bushwalking and you are on your way back to your car. You're feeling hot and tired and it is a relief to see the car in the distance. As you walk towards it, you suddenly realise that a snake lays coiled on the path ahead of you. The snake is between you and your car. You stop and look for a way around the snake, but there isn't one, just dense bush on either side of the walking track. You have no doubt that other snakes would be in the undergrowth. You wait for a while, hoping that someone will come and help you, but no one does.

You begin to walk towards the snake, with slow measured steps. Your heart is pounding as you get closer to it. It doesn't move. You look around for a detour from the path, but again you can't find one. You are surrounded by dense bush to the left and right of you. You stop again. The snake doesn't move.

You creep closer and closer to it. On which side should you pass the snake? If it hears you and takes flight, which way will it go? To the left or to the right? What if it goes straight ahead, down the path towards your car? What if it hears you and strikes out of fear? What can you do?

Your heart is pounding so hard, you are sure the snake will hear it. Your breathing is fast and shallow. You are perspiring, and it is not from the heat of the sun but as a result of your fear.

You have almost reached the snake. Your whole body is responding to the threat. You stop again, take a deep breath and hold it. You wait for the snake to move. It doesn't. You take another step, and the snake still doesn't move. You are now almost beside the snake. You look at it closely, and you realise it is simply a piece of rope someone has dropped on the path.

How many times have we done something like this? Not so much with snakes and pieces of rope, but there would have been occasions when you saw something and it turns out it isn't what you first thought it was. When driving on a hot day, for example, it appears as if there is water on the road but it turns out to be a mirage. It is just the heat shimmering on the hot surface.

What about the three-dimensional pictures that everyone had a few years ago? Some of us could look at the images and pick up the 'hidden' picture behind it almost straight away. Other people had to take a closer look before the picture became obvious.

So too with our panic attacks and our anxiety. We *perceive* our attacks and anxiety as being something other than what they are. We perceive our symptoms as being life threatening or a threat to our sanity, or a sign that we are about to lose control in some way. While our symptoms can feel very ferocious, they are not signs of anything other than what they are: symptoms of our panic attacks and anxiety. They are *not* what we *perceive* them to be. This is how we are 'supposed' to feel when we dissociate, or have a panic attack or feel anxious.

It is our fear of our symptoms that is the driving force of panic disorder. Lose the fear and we 'lose' the disorder, with its many secondary fears and associated anxiety. This also applies to social anxiety, obsessive compulsive disorder and generalised anxiety disorder. This does not mean we will never be anxious, or never dissociate or never have an attack again. But once we lose our fear, we simply don't care if we dissociate or have an attack occasionally. 'So what!' We know them for what they are. A trance state, a panic attack – nothing more. If we feel anxious, we need to see what the anxiety is telling us. Because the more mindful we become, we will see that our anxiety will always be telling us something.

Recovery is a change of *perception*. That word 'perception' is so important. It is our perception of our anxiety and panic attacks that needs to change. Not only do we need to change the way we think about our attacks and anxiety, we need to change the way we see them – the way we perceive them to be. When we can see them as they are, and for what they are, our thinking changes accordingly and we lose our fear of them.

To repeat what I have said in earlier chapters, we need to bring our emotional development to the level of our intellectual development. Intellectually we see them for what they are, but we are still trapped in the disorder because at an emotional level we do not believe they won't hurt us.

SO WHAT!

Working with a mindfulness cognitive technique enables us to see at an emotional level why there is nothing to fear from our attacks or anxiety. This is the power – to see it and to understand why there is nothing to fear. This is why so many of us can now say 'So what!' if we have an attack or if we become anxious.

Before we begin to work with a mindfulness technique, it is

difficult to grasp the significance of 'So what!' because we are caught up in the horror of our experience. 'So what!' is a state of mind. It is the end result of working with a mindfulness technique. 'So what!' is the acknowledgement and emotional recognition that our attacks and anxiety are simply that, an attack or anxiety. Nothing more. When we are caught up in our fears and our disorder, we are not seeing or accepting the reality of our experience.

MIND STATES

The reality is that nothing happens to us as a result of our attacks and anxiety. Our life as we knew it can be destroyed by our 'What if . . .?' and similar thinking, but our worst fears do not come true. When I say this in my workshops, I can tell by the expression on everyone's face that they don't believe me. Everyone is thinking to themselves, 'It is going to be me. I am going to be the one who will die from it, go insane from it, lose control in some way.'

But as I always say, 'Why will *you* be the first one this is going to happen to? Why will *you* be the first one to be written about in all the medical journals as being "the one it happened to"?' Our thought that 'I will be the one' is just another thought. But we unknowingly give our thoughts the power to destroy our lives.

It is the way we perceive and think about our experience that disables us and creates havoc in our lives. It is not our attacks or our anxiety; it is our fear of them.

Our various mind states – that is, the way we think – turn on the fight and flight response, and our symptoms of panic and anxiety are the result. Or we may dissociate and then become caught up in our thoughts, which then turn on the fight and flight response, which again creates our anxiety and panic.

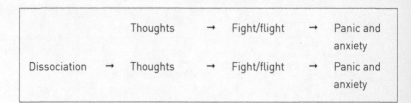

Most of us realise and acknowledge how negative our thoughts are, and we know at one level how our thoughts are creating our distress. But there is a 'gap' between knowing this and working effectively with our thinking. We can try various techniques – positive thinking, distraction techniques or realistic thinking – but many of us can't cross over the divide and stop the many and varied fears we have. We keep getting caught up in the overall experience of our disorder. What we don't realise is that we have become caught up in our various mind states.

Our mind moves in and out of different mind states. And our thoughts create all our feeling states – our happiness, sadness, anger, boredom, depression, excitement, irritability, hopefulness, helplessness, panic, anxiety, fear and *freedom*. We don't realise that we move in and out of these feeling states, guided by the way we are thinking. And we can move in and out of these feeling states from moment to moment.

One moment we can be feeling happy and a thought arises, 'I am feeling so good.' This is followed by another thought about feelings of happiness not lasting, and we become anxious or depressed. Then we think, 'I knew it wouldn't last!' and we become attached to associated thoughts: 'Why does this always happen to me? Why can't I be happy?' We become a participant in our mind states.

Our mind states

Anxiety

I don't want to have another panic attack	What if do have one?
What's my heart rate?	It's always too fast
This is not me, I'm not like this	Why can't I recover?
I hate feeling like this	I don't want to be like this
Why doesn't it just go away?	I feel so horrible
What if something does happen?	Why do I feel this way?
I feel so awful	I can't feel like this
I shouldn't feel this way	Who wouldn't be anxious?
I can't keep feeling this way	Why can't I stop this?
No one else could feel this way	I can't cope

What if . . .

The doctor has made a mistake?	This is a brain tumour?
There really is something wrong?	I have a heart attack?
This isn't anxiety?	I go insane?
I have an attack?	The next one is the big one?
The test results were mixed up?	I make a fool of myself?
I lose control?	I have an attack of diarrhoea?
I vomit?	I feel dizzy, pass out or faint?
They see my hands shake?	No one is there to help me?
I blush?	I perspire too much?

I never recover?

People think I am a fraud?

I am at work and have to leave?

I get home and I am alone?

I can't get help?

People find out about me?

I can't get to work?

I can't get home?

I have an attack in the car?

Something happens?

Sleep

I can't sleep

How can I function tomorrow?

What will happen if I get no sleep?

I have to sleep

Why isn't it happening?

I am going to feel so bad in the morning

What will happen to me if I don't get to sleep?

What if tonight is like last night?

What if I wake up in a couple of hours?

I can't function if I don't sleep

I'm trying to sleep but can't

I need my sleep

How can I cope?

I have to make sure I go to sleep

Mental abuse

I am a failure

I am weak

I hate myself

I should be able to get it together

I am to blame

I am hopeless

I am stupid

Why can't I be strong enough?

I am angry at myself

It's all my fault

Check mate

I should	I shouldn't
I must	I have to
I can't	I must do it perfectly
I should recover	I shouldn't feel like this
I must recover	I have to recover
I can't cope	I can't be selfish

Guilt

I shouldn't have done that	I shouldn't have said that
I should have said yes	Why am I so selfish?
I didn't mean to hurt their feelings	What if they misunderstood me?
I am such a bad person	I should have done it better
I shouldn't be angry	It is all my fault
I am letting everyone down	Why am I such a terrible person?

Victim

I am worse than everyone else	I can never recover
No one else is as bad as I am	I am a failure
It is just not fair I am like this	Why me?

This is how we think between our attacks, and this is what creates our anxiety and feelings of loss of control over our lives. But we haven't lost control; we have become attached to our thoughts.

And sometimes the remedies we try to stop these mind states just keep them all going.

POSITIVE THINKING – AFFIRMATIONS

'Every day in every way I am getting better and better.'

We can write down this and other affirmations, and put them on the bedroom mirror, on top of the television, in the hallway, on the refrigerator. In fact we can wallpaper our whole house with them. We are constantly reminded of them, because they are everywhere. We repeat them to ourselves ad nauseam, but it doesn't work.

'Every day in every way we are getting sicker and sicker!'

'Every day in every way I am getting better and better . . . what's my pulse rate? Has it gone down? My heart is still racing, I hate feeling like this, why doesn't it just go away? Every day in every way I am feeling better and better. What if I have an attack, what if I have a heart attack? Every day in every way . . .'

POSITIVE THINKING – NEGATIVE THINKING

We can repeat affirmations and replace negative thoughts with positive ones, but sometimes it's to no avail. I think that positive thinking can sometimes be as destructive as negative thinking. Most of us do not believe the 'positive' because of the way we perceive our panic attacks and anxiety. Our internal conversation can be:

'I feel fantastic. No, *you* feel terrible. I feel great. Are *you* kidding? You feel horrible. I know today is going to be a wonderful day. For *you* or for your anxiety? I am never going to panic again. Want to make a bet?'

DISTRACTION

Some people use distraction techniques, but they don't last. Nor do they bridge the gap of knowing and working effectively with our thinking, because we are not dealing with the root cause of our distress, and that is the thoughts themselves.

'I'm feeling really anxious. I can't feel like this. I'll count to twenty. One, two, three – that isn't working. I'll concentrate really hard on this book I'm reading. No, that isn't working. I feel terrible, I'll watch television. No, I still feel awful. I will go for a walk, smell the roses so to speak – but what if I have a panic attack on the way?'

REALISTIC THINKING

This can also happen sometimes using other cognitive techniques such as realistic thinking. With this technique we write down our thoughts and find the evidence that proves or disproves the thought, and then write down a more realistic-based thought next to our panic/anxiety ones.

Thought: 'I am going to go insane.'
Where is the evidence that proves this? 'I haven't gone insane . . . yet.'
Where is the evidence that proves I won't? 'My doctor and other people say that I won't go insane. No one goes insane through an anxiety disorder . . . But are they really sure?'

Realistic thought: 'My panic and anxiety will not send me insane (well, at least I hope it won't).'

ANALYSIS

We can also write down all of our thoughts. In fact, we could fill book after book with them. And we can analyse them, and analyse them, and become trapped in analysis paralysis, and around and around we go.

'Look at all these thoughts. Why am I thinking like this? Why am I having these thoughts? There has to be a reason. What is wrong with me? The answer has to be here some- where. Why can't I work out why I am thinking like this? It is driving me crazy. I hate this. Why is this happening to me? Why doesn't it just stop and go away? It is nonstop over and over again. Why am I thinking like this? 'Every day in every way . . . One. Two. Three. I can't find the evidence that I won't go insane!'

CHAPTER 12

Mindfulness as a cognitive technique

As I have been saying, the way we are thinking is creating our anxiety and panic symptoms. When we fear our symptoms, or try to stop them, all we are doing is creating more.

We are not aware of the enormous power our thoughts have. It is our thoughts that generate our feelings and emotions. We don't recognise how we can be happy one moment, anxious the next, feeling guilty the next, and feeling helpless the next. We simply don't recognise the power of thought and how our thoughts dictate the feeling quality of our life. We attach to our thoughts from the moment we wake in the morning, and we remain caught up in them until we go to sleep at night.

When we begin to meditate, we become much more aware of our thoughts. As our meditation deepens, we become aware and see how our thoughts are not an endless stream, but rise independently of each other. A thought rises into consciousness and if we don't attach to it, it will subside. Another thought will rise, then dissolve. This is the nature of our mind. The rising and falling away of thoughts. Like the rising of a wave in the ocean, the wave peaks and then dissolves back into the ocean.

But we don't let our thoughts dissolve. We attach to them and we are carried along with the tide, not realising that our thoughts are constantly rising and falling away. We are a participant in our states of our mind, and we are not aware of how these states determine the quality of our life.

CHANGING OUR PERCEPTION

If we read through all the mind states listed in Chapter 11, we can see how we are not dealing with the current moment in time. We miss the current moment because we are either thinking of past experiences and/or projecting into the future. We are not aware of how memories or thoughts of the past cause much of our suffering in the present moment. This in turn contaminates the future, which, incidentally, is only a moment away.

To begin to work with our thinking, we need to come to the current moment and work with our disorder as it is in this moment. Let's come back to basics. When we had our first few attacks, or began to experience high levels of anxiety, we were frightened and confused. We did not know what was happening to us and that is completely understandable. It is a terrifying experience.

But now we know what is happening. We have had all the necessary clinical tests, and we have been diagnosed as having an anxiety disorder. It doesn't mean we are having a heart attack, nor does it mean we are going to die or go insane or lose control in some way. It means we are having panic attacks and/or anxiety. This is how we are *supposed to feel* when we have them. Nothing more, nothing less. This is the reality of our experience in this moment in time.

Yet, we are not dealing with them in this moment. Nor are we dealing with them as they really are. We draw on our past experiences of our attacks, anxiety and feelings of terror, and project them into the future. Whether that be in the next moment or five minutes or five days or more away.

The first step in changing our perception is for us to begin again in this moment. To do this, we need to let go of our past experiences of our attacks and anxiety, and the numerous fears we may have. We will not be able to begin again if we use our past experiences as a frame of reference, because this is already determining our future. We can change the future by changing our frame of reference – that is, the way we perceive our attacks and anxiety. We let go of past experiences and begin again, right now in this moment.

In building a new frame of reference, we bring into this moment the fact that our major panic and anxiety fears have not happened, nor will they happen as a result of panic and anxiety. We may occasionally have felt embarrassed or felt we made a fool of ourselves, but nothing has happened to us.

Our lives as we knew them may have been destroyed by our anxiety disorder, but they have been destroyed more by our *perception* of our panic attacks and anxiety than by the actual experience of them. If we didn't fear them, we would not be experiencing the distress that we do. We need to begin again, and learn to understand why our fears about our panic and anxiety will not happen now or in the future.

We need to be mindful of our thoughts, and we need to become aware of how our thoughts are creating our feeling states. In this instance, if we experience panic disorder, we need to become aware of:

- any ability to dissociate

- how this in turn can trigger a panic attack
- how our thoughts trigger the fight-or-flight response
- how this response creates our feelings of panic and anxiety

If we experience one of the other anxiety disorders, we need to become aware of:

- how our thoughts trigger the fight-or-flight response
- how this response creates our feelings of panic and anxiety

When we can see how our experience is being created, we realise why there is nothing to fear. Our perception of our experience changes. Our attitude towards our symptoms changes. We see this not just at an intellectual level but, most importantly, we see it at an emotional level. When we can see and feel how it is all being created, we lose our fear because we understand it and we understand why it will not hurt us. When we can see and feel the truth of this at an emotional level, we take back the power!

BEGINNING AGAIN

In meditation, we learn to become mindful – aware of when we are attaching to our thoughts rather than focusing on the object of meditation. We bring this same principle into everyday life, except this time we will not be meditating; we will be using mindfulness as a cognitive technique. We simply become mindful of our thoughts and the feeling states that arise from these thoughts. Becoming mindful means we separate ourselves from our thoughts; we step back from our thoughts and simply watch them, become aware of them. At this stage, we become a spectator, not a participant, in our mind states. We observe our thoughts, we witness our thoughts.

We need to observe the whole thought process. When we feel anxious, we don't see the thought that turned on the fight-or-flight response. Instead, we go immediately to the feeling of being anxious, and think anxiously about it. We don't see the mind state that originally created it, because we have become caught up, attached to the very act of thinking. In becoming mindful, we break our attachment to the thinking process and simply become aware of the process itself.

MINDFULNESS AS A COGNITIVE TECHNIQUE

We need to be aware; we need to be mindful of what we are thinking about. We need to watch the moment-to-moment passing parade of our thoughts. It is not a matter of analysing them or wondering why we are thinking like this. It is not a matter of telling ourselves, I shouldn't think this. We need to be mindful, and we need to be non-judgmental. The more mindful we can become, the more we will begin to see the dynamics of our whole experience.

As we begin to practise becoming mindful, it is very easy for us to forget about being aware and to attach back into our thoughts. This is where we need to become disciplined, and it can be helpful if we use reminders throughout the day to assist us in becoming aware of what we are thinking about.

What are you thinking of when you:

- wake in the morning?
- have breakfast?
- begin the day?
- take the children to school?
- leave for work?
- see a bus?
- see a red car?
- hear the phone ring?

- have morning tea?
- have lunch?
- have afternoon tea?
- come home?
- have dinner?
- go for a walk?
- prepare a meal?
- feed your pets?
- wash the dishes?
- prepare for a social occasion?
- are at a social occasion?
- come home after a social occasion?
- prepare for a business meeting?
- are at a meeting?
- come out of a meeting?
- help the children with their homework?
- settle the children for the night?
- watch television?
- turn on the computer?
- get ready for bed?

What are you thinking about right now?

We need to listen to our thoughts and become aware of our own mind states, aware of the incessant internal conversations. *Something may have happened, or could happen, or shouldn't happen.* Watch the thoughts as they weave various conversations, various outcomes, round and round.

Become aware of how you switch on the 'radar' first thing in the morning to see if your symptoms are awake. And of course they are, because the moment you turn on the radar, they are ready for the day's action!

DISSOCIATION

If you have any of the dissociative symptoms listed in Chapter 5, become aware of how they are happening. How did you move into a trance state?

- Were you staring?
- What were you staring at?
  - out of the window
  - while driving the car
  - stopped at a red light
  - the car in front of you
  - the road ahead of you
  - the computer
  - the television
  - a book
- Were you talking with someone?
- Were you daydreaming? If so, how deep was the daydream state?
- Were you totally absorbed in your thinking?
- Were you totally absorbed in a creative project?
- Were you under fluorescent lights?
- Other _____

The more aware we become, the more we will recognise the sequence of events that lead to our overall experience.

Dissociation with anxiety

Cause: Staring or self-absorption or fluorescent lights
Effect: Dissociation/trance state – fearful anxious thoughts – fight-or-flight response – anxiety symptoms – thoughts – fight and flight response . . .

Dissociation with a panic attack

Cause: Staring or self absorption or fluorescent lights
Effect: Dissociation/trance state – thoughts – fight-or-flight response – panic anxiety symptoms – thoughts – fight-or-flight response . . .

Nocturnal panic attack

Cause: Change in consciousness during sleep
Effect: Attack – thoughts – fight-or-flight response – panic and anxiety symptoms – thoughts – fight-or-flight response . . .

Panic attacks without dissociation

Cause: Thoughts
Effect: Fight-or-flight response – panic and anxiety symptoms – thoughts – fight-or-flight response . . .

Anxiety

Cause: Thoughts
Effect: Fight-or-flight response – symptoms – thoughts – fight-or-flight response . . .

MINDFULNESS CHECK LIST 1

Dissociative/trance states

- What were you doing before you dissociated?
- How did you dissociate?
- What were you thinking about when you dissociated?
- What happened the moment you tranced? What did you think?

- Did you panic?
- If so, what were you thinking about?

Panic attacks/anxiety

- What were you thinking about just before your last panic attack?
- What were you thinking about during your last panic attack?
- What were you thinking about after your last panic attack?
- What were you thinking about before your anxiety peaked to higher levels?
- What were you thinking about after your anxiety peaked to higher levels?
- What are you thinking about when you are chronically anxious every waking moment?
- What were you thinking about as you woke up this morning?
- What were you thinking about as you went to sleep last night?
- What were you thinking about shortly before you realised you were feeling depressed?
- What did you think about when you realised you were feeling depressed?
- Do you become depressed because you are feeling depressed?
- What thoughts created the depression over the depression?

The answer is not: 'I wasn't thinking of anything or doing anything.' You were! You are just not aware.

When we attach to our thoughts we don't recognise that we are thinking, because we are caught up in the very act of thinking. There is no separation between thinker and thought. And so we lose the clarity of what is actually happening in the present moment. We allow a mental process to dictate the way we feel, not just in the present moment but also into the future.

In the initial stages of becoming mindful, we get caught up time and again in any dissociation and/or in our thoughts, and before we know it we are panicking or highly anxious. We need to become disciplined in becoming mindful. It is very important that we become aware of the intimate connection between our dissociation and our attack, and/or the connection between our thoughts and feelings of panic and anxiety. Until we see this connection, we will remain fearful of our experience.

We need to be aware of how it is being created, moment to moment. And when we can see this both intellectually and emotionally, we realise there is nothing to be afraid of, and our fears dissolve.

Many people tell me that they can't bear to be aware of their thoughts because they are so relentless and negative. The reason why our thoughts come so relentlessly is because we are attaching to them, including the thought that we shouldn't have these thoughts! It doesn't matter if we have a negative thought. We are going to. We all do. The secret is not to worry if we do. When we judge our thoughts as being 'negative', we give our power away. It is the judgment that does the damage: 'Why am I thinking like this. Why doesn't it go away? What do I have to do to stop it? I shouldn't think like this!' This is how our mind keeps reinventing itself, from moment to moment.

Just watch, be aware. Don't judge. Simply watch the rise and fall of thoughts. Anxiety thought, panic thought, depressive thought, negative thought, happy thought, curious thought.

We can watch our thoughts as we would watch a street parade. Clowns, marching bands, people dressed in various costumes. We watch the parade, but we don't take part in it. And this is what we need to do with our thoughts. Just let them pass by. Nor is there a reason to fear our thoughts. See them for what they are. Thoughts. Nothing more. *We give them the power by fearing them.* When we can detach from our thoughts and simply watch them, they will disappear and take our symptoms with them.

Trying to replace 'negative' thoughts with 'positive' ones or trying to distract from them is trying to change the 'rules' of that particular mind state. And the mind will not allow us to do that. So we need to become a spectator and simply watch from the sidelines. When we don't hook into the thoughts, they simply rise into consciousness and then disappear. It is the attaching to particular thoughts that gives rise to similar thoughts.

We also need to realise that when we become aware, we actually see the whole process for the first time. These thoughts have always been around, but now we are seeing them. People can become frightened of seeing the content of their thoughts. They will push them away, turn off their awareness and think I can't think about this, I don't want to know this. But what happens? The thoughts are still there and are still creating the problem. Being frightened of them, not wanting to know about them, keeps the cycle going.

MINDFULNESS CHECK LIST 2

- What is the relationship between any ability to dissociate and your panic attack sensations?
- What is the relationship between your thoughts and your anxiety, panic or depression?
- Can you see how your thoughts are creating the fear?
- Can you see how your body reacts to the fear?
- Can you see why there is nothing to be frightened of?
- What difficulties are you having?

- Are you having difficulty in becoming aware?
- Are you attaching to all of your thoughts?
- Are you frightened of your thoughts?
- Do you think, 'I can't do this'?
- Do you think, 'This is all too hard'?
- Do you feel your thoughts are racing too fast to do this?
- Are you thinking, 'I shouldn't be thinking like this'?

These are just thoughts! Step back and simply let your thoughts parade by.

Letting go of thoughts

When we learn to become mindful, we separate ourselves from our thoughts. Instead of attaching to them, we simply observe them. We see how our thoughts turn on the fight-or-flight response, and we see how our symptoms are being created. As we become more familiar with the overall relationship between our thoughts and symptoms, we realise that we can actually have a choice in what we think about.

We know that if we continue with a particular thought pattern, we will become caught up in a mind state that can lead to anxiety, panic or depression. We can choose to keep on thinking the thoughts, or we can choose to let them go. And to 'let them go', we draw on the meditation technique again.

In meditation we are aware when we become involved with our thoughts, and we let the thoughts go and bring our mind back to the object of our meditation. In everyday living we change this slightly. While we will still be letting go of our thoughts, we will not be bringing our mind back to a word or breath or image. Instead, we will label the thought, and then we will let it go.

We label our thoughts for three reasons.

1. It helps us to recognise the various types of thoughts that we have, and how these create our feeling states.
2. To break our attachment to the thought. When we exercise our choice and choose not to become involved in a particular thought pattern, we take back the power.
3. It prevents us from distracting from them. When we label the thought, we acknowledge it. We are not 'running' from it.

   This can happen when we distract from our thoughts. If we distract, we are not given the opportunity to understand exactly how our thoughts are creating our experience. Nor does it give us an opportunity to learn how to control our thoughts.

We become aware of our thoughts, we choose not to think them and so we:

1. Label the thought:

Anxiety	Panic	Depression
Guilt	Victim	What will people think
Frustrated	Negative	Mental abuse

Other_____

We don't run from our thought, or avoid it, or change it, or analyse it or judge it. When we do any of these, all we are doing is giving our thoughts the power and we become caught up yet again.

Some people wonder if labelling our thoughts is being negative.

It isn't. Labelling our thoughts is not judging; it is acknowledging them. Judging our thoughts is fear-based. Labelling our thoughts enables us to let them go more easily. When we judge our thoughts, it is difficult to let them go.

Don't become caught up in 'What should I label this thought?' If you are not sure what type of thought it is, label it a 'negative' thought and let it go.

Once we label the thought, we simply:

2. Let it go as we do in meditation

We *do not* bring our mind back to a word or breath or image. Instead, we become involved in labelling our thoughts and letting them go. The moment we label our thoughts and let them go, they will come straight back. We let that thought go and it will come up again immediately. We label it and let it go.

We need to remember that our mind is not disciplined. It runs free – free to create havoc in our lives! It is not going to hand over the control to us easily. In the beginning, our thoughts will win. We will attach to them, and get caught up in them time and again. And so we need patience and more patience! We are training our mind to perceive and to think another way, so it is going to take time.

In time, with practice and discipline, our thoughts will rise into consciousness and automatically disappear without our need to let them go. At this stage we will have total and complete power over our thoughts. If we want to think about something, we consciously choose to. Otherwise our thoughts disappear without any effort on our part.

Before we move to the next point let's summarise where we are:

- We need to become aware of any ability to dissociate
- We need to become aware, to be mindful of our thoughts

- We need to become aware of what we are thinking about
- We need to become aware of how our body is reacting to our thoughts
- We need to be aware that we have a choice in what we think about
- We can keep thinking our thoughts, or
- We can label them and let them go

MINDFULNESS CHECK LIST 3

Are you having difficulty in letting your thoughts go? Do you:

- Find you are constantly getting caught up in your thoughts?
- Think you will never be able to control them?
- Think your thoughts have a life of their own?
- Think it all seems to difficult?

Remember these are also just thoughts!

3. Letting it happen

Becoming aware of cause and effect – that is, the relationship between any dissociation, our thoughts and our symptoms and/ or our thoughts and symptoms – shows us very clearly how our distress is being created. The more we understand this, the more our perception of our experience changes and it becomes easier to control our thoughts.

As we are learning to be aware of our thoughts and learning to let them go, we will still have symptoms, because we will still be getting caught up in our thoughts. And so the next step is taking back our power by letting our panic and anxiety happen. This means we stop fighting them.

When we don't know or understand what is happening to us, it is only natural that we fight it. But now that we do know, we need to stop *fighting* it. This only makes the situation worse. When we fight and resist our symptoms, we keep the fight and flight response activated.

- We fight it mentally: 'Oh no, not again.' 'I hate this.' 'I can't stand it.' 'Why doesn't it go away?'
- We fight it by monitoring: 'Where is it? 'What's my heart rate?' 'Are my hands shaking?'
- We fight it physically: we hold our breath, tense our muscles, clench our fists or our jaw.

But what is our fighting doing? Is it *helping* in anyway? No it isn't. If fighting it was going to stop it, we wouldn't have a disorder in the first place!

We need to let our symptoms happen without fighting them. To do this, we come back to the practice of meditation. We have already brought over from our meditation practice the skills of being aware and of letting go of our thoughts. Now we need to bring over the skill of letting ourselves feel whatever it is we are feeling. In meditation we simply let whatever happens, happen. We don't fight it in any way. We don't resist it in any way. Nor do we control it in any way. We just let whatever happens, happen. We need to bring this skill into our everyday life.

What did you think when you read that you need to let the panic attacks and the symptoms of anxiety happen? Did you think, 'I can't do that? What will happen? How can I let that happen?' How did you respond physically? Did you feel anxious? You probably did. Most people do when they hear this. Did the anxiety or the negative thoughts come first? You'll find that the thoughts came first, and the symptoms followed.

If we dissociate, then it is a matter of being aware how we are dissociating, of breaking our stare, breaking our gaze or breaking our self-absorption and letting go of any fearful thoughts about it. 'So what!'

If we have an attack we need to let it happen. To let it do whatever it wants to do. If we have an electric shock move through our body, then we let it move through. If we have the sensation of burning heat or a burning tingling heat, a vibration or unusual energies moving through our body, then we let it happen. 'So what!' If we are woken from sleep with a nocturnal attack, all it means is that it has woken us. Let it happen – 'So what!' – and roll over and go back to sleep.

We simply don't resist it or fight whatever we experience. We give into it. Instead of 'What if . . .?', we need to see it for what it is. So what!'

When we are having a panic attack that has been induced by our thoughts, we let the panic attack happen without fighting it or resisting it. If we feel anxious, we let ourselves feel anxious. If we are hyperventilating, we break the hyperventilation.

Once we have been told by our doctor that there is nothing wrong with our heart, and if our heart is racing through the anxiety, then we simply note it, 'heart racing', and we let it race. If we are feeling nauseous, then we let ourselves feel nauseous; if we are going to be sick, then we let ourselves be sick. If we are going to have an attack of diarrhoea, then we have an attack of diarrhoea. If we need to urinate, then we need to urinate. If our hands are shaking, then our hands are shaking. If our face is flushed, then our face is flushed. If we are perspiring, then we are perspiring. If we feel as if we are going to faint, then we sit down – on a chair, on the floor or on the footpath if need be.

We simply don't resist or fight whatever we experience. We give into it. Instead of 'What if . . .?', we learn to say, and to believe, 'So what!'

Now I know what you are thinking! After this session in my workshops, people queue up to say to me in hushed whispers, 'I can't let it happen. What would people think? I am a nurse/teacher/CEO/lawyer/marketing manager/bank officer/waiter/cashier/student. What would people say? They can't see me have an attack. I can't let my hands shake, I can't be sick, I can't have an attack of diarrhoea, I can't have a flushed face, I can't be soaked through with perspiration.'

Why not? If it means you'll recover, so what!

It doesn't matter what other people think. Think about it. Our mental health needs to be more important than what we think other people are thinking! Our recovery needs to be our number one priority. Many of us are the greatest actors in the world. No one would know if we were having an attack or feeling anxious. We are experts in being able to hide it. But how much energy does it take to do this? It takes an enormous amount, and all this does is keep the fight and flight response going.

We don't realise that when we are worrying about what other people think, they may not be thinking anything about us at all! We hide it from other people and my rule of thumb is three people who we know are hiding it from us for the same reason we are hiding it from them: 'What will they think of me?'

Our mental health is more important than what we perceive other people's opinions to be. The irony is the harder we fight our experience, the more we fuel it. There is more chance of someone seeing physical signs of our panic and anxiety when we fight it. When we let it happen, we turn off the fight and flight response and it is over as quickly as it started. Instead of 'What if . . .?' it becomes 'So what!'

CASE HISTORIES

Sally

Sally was in a supermarket one Friday after work. She'd had a tough week and was feeling tired and anxious. She just wanted to get her groceries and leave. Suddenly she saw a friend walking towards her, smiling. She thought to herself, 'Oh, no. I don't want to talk to anyone. I just feel so awful.' She forced herself to exchange pleasantries and asked her friend, 'So how are you?' Her friend gave her the automatic polite response. 'Fine, fine. How are you?'

Sally paused. Her friend had a full trolley and seemed preoccupied with her to-do list. Sally took the plunge and replied truthfully, 'I don't know. I'm having such a difficult time with this anxiety. When I saw you I thought I might have a panic attack because I haven't got the energy to try and hide it.'

Sally waited for the uncomfortable silence, or for her friend to mumble an excuse and make for the check-outs, but was surprised when her friend responded immediately with, 'That's good. Glad to hear it.'

Sally couldn't believe it. Her friend hadn't even been listening! Her friend was on automatic pilot, caught up with her own thoughts. She'd heard what she expected to hear, that Sally was fine!

We just let our panic attacks or anxiety happen. We do not need to become involved with them. When we are feeling happy, what do we do? Do we monitor our body for happiness? My head is happy. My throat is happy, my heart is happy, my stomach is happy, my bowel is happy, my bladder is happy. Of course we don't. We simply note that we are happy and get on with what we are doing (as long as we are not thinking, 'How long will this last?').

The same applies to our panic and anxiety. We don't need to become caught up in it, or caught up in the thoughts that created it. We choose not to become involved with our thoughts; we label them, let them go and let our symptoms happen.

What we don't realise is that when we let the anxiety and attacks happen, the only thing that happens to us is we recover! When we let it happen and don't buy into it with our thinking, when we don't resist it, we turn off the fight-or-flight response and it stops. It is over, because there is nothing to fuel it, unless we think to ourselves, 'what if?'

It can be frightening the first time we let it happen, because we are taking our major fears head-on. But we allow ourselves to feel frightened and we let it happen! 'So what!'

To summarise:

- We need to become aware of any ability to dissociate
- If we have dissociated we need to break it as I have outlined above

And/or

- We need to become aware, to be mindful of our thoughts.
- We need to be mindful of how our body is reacting to our thoughts
- We need to be aware that we have a choice in what we think about
- We can keep thinking our thoughts or we can label them and let them go.
- We let our panic attacks and anxiety happen

RECOVERY WITH ATTITUDE

Our anger is far more powerful than our anxiety and panic, and it can be the 'rocket ship' to recovery. We all have problems experiencing our anger; this is part of the reason why we have developed the disorder in the first place! But there comes a time, as we are working through the recovery process, that we do feel angry. Angry at being mindful and angry about labelling and letting go of our thoughts. We think to ourselves, enough is enough!

Some people will become angry at themselves. We need to direct our anger at our thoughts, our symptoms, and at everything associated with our disorder rather than ourselves. Being angry at ourselves will only create further anxiety and panic. We need to separate ourselves from our anxiety disorder. We are not an anxiety disorder – we are a person who has one. It is happening to us. It is like a person with a broken leg. They don't turn into a broken leg; they *have* a broken leg.

Sometimes it is difficult to see this separation, because we can be so caught up in it all. It is the same with our thoughts. Our thoughts are now part and parcel of the disorder. They are not us. We can separate ourselves away from them.

Get angry at the thoughts that create the disorder. Get angry at the anxiety, the panic, and the avoidance behaviour. How dare it do this to you! How dare it destroy your life! Enough is enough is enough! Tell it where to go in whatever language you feel comfortable with. For me, it was what one psychiatrist calls Bronwyn's 'F' technique!

Why aren't we angry? Our disorder can take over and destroy our life as we knew it. We can hate our disorder, but no matter how much we 'hate' it, we are still passive in our response to it. Why? Anger is a healthy response to what is happening to us. If someone broke into our home and stole our most treasured possessions, would our reaction be a passive one? Would we blame ourselves? Or would we be angry?

ANGER CHECK LIST

- Why aren't you angry at your disorder?
- Are you frightened to feel the anger?
- Are you directing the anger back on to yourself or other people?
- Do you think that if you get angry you will lose control?
- Do you think that you are not an angry person so you can't get angry?
- Why aren't you angry about what has happened to you?

When we are angry and we direct that anger at our disorder, we need to do it with power. Not 'go away I am angry at you' but '**GO AWAY**' or words to that effect! Feel the full extent of your anger and feel its power. You will know when you are doing it the right way, because your anxiety and panic will disappear so fast that it can be frightening! It's the same with your thoughts. Tell them in no uncertain terms what to do.

Take back the power!

Part 4

Working through to recovery

CHAPTER 13

The layers of recovery

Skilful action is:
- Being open to the idea of caring and accepting ourselves as we are right now
- Becoming responsible for ourselves
- Accepting our anxiety disorder
- Understanding our disorder
- Becoming disciplined in meditation or another relaxation technique
- Developing mindfulness cognitive skills

This enables us to work through the process of recovery by:
- Learning to manage our panic attacks and anxiety on a daily basis
- Working with our avoidance behaviour
- Working through any prescribed drug addiction or alcohol dependency
- Choosing to work through any unresolved past or current personal issues, including any history of childhood abuse

- Choosing to work towards building our self-esteem

I use the word 'choosing' in the last two points because some people will go on to work with their self-esteem issues and, if applicable, any history of childhood abuse, but other people might prefer not to. There is no right or wrong way. The bottom line is doing what we feel is most beneficial for us as individuals. But if we don't work with the other points listed above, we will not learn to manage our attacks and anxiety.

THRESHOLD TO STRESS

When I ask people what happened in their life prior to developing an anxiety disorder, they usually list a number of major stressful events. Some of these may have occurred six to twelve months before their disorder was triggered.

During one of my workshops, a woman listed a number of stressful events she had experienced in the past year. A family member had died; she and her partner had bought a new house; she had been retrenched from her employment a couple of months later; their children were having difficulty adjusting to a new suburb and school; and her partner had been injured in a car accident. When I asked her if she could see the relationship between these events and the development of her panic attacks, she replied that she should have been able to deal with all of it without it affecting her!

We expect nothing less from ourselves, and then we can't understand why we develop a disorder. We think we should just get on with it, and 'get on with it' as perfectly as possible.

Would you expect other people to deal with major stress without any effect? Would you tell them they are weak or a failure?

Would you tell them they should pull themselves together so they can be strong for other people? Would you say this to someone else? No, of course not. So why are you expecting this of yourself?

CASE HISTORIES

Betty

Betty had worked extremely hard on her recovery. She had been able to return to work three months ago and was really happy to be back in the work force. Although she'd had the occasional bad day, she was able to work through them and she had begun to feel that she had finally recovered. That was until last week.

Now Betty was beginning to think the disorder was returning. Her anxiety was increasing and the attacks had returned. She knew that going back to work had been stressful, but she was happy in her job. She couldn't understand why the anxiety and the attacks were back. To all intents and purposes life was normal. Her husband and children were fine. Although Betty realised it was hard to run a household and work at the same time, she felt it was worth the extra effort. Her father's death two months ago had been traumatic but she felt that couldn't be the reason. Betty wondered if it was the argument she had had with her mother and sisters. The issues had still not been resolved, and each time they were together the atmosphere was quite tense. She knew the anxiety and the attacks were making her feel tense, but she couldn't understand why they had come back. Betty thought she needed to be more aware of what was causing stress in her life.

David

David had been making little progress with his recovery and was becoming disillusioned with the recovery program. He was having difficulty finding the time to concentrate on his recovery. There were so many other things that needed to be done first. He had volunteered to take on extra duties at work because of staff shortages, which meant he wasn't getting home until 7 p.m. Working late meant he spent less time with his children, so he did his best to make up for it on weekends. This interfered with the work he did for two service clubs in his area, but he tried to juggle his time. This in turn was complicated by the fact that his neighbours and friends were always dropping by with various requests for favours or help. On top of all this he had to stop and take time out when the anxiety and the attacks became too much. Having to find time to work on his recovery was the final straw. David was feeling quite resentful because he thought there should be some sort of recovery program that took all of these demands on his time into account.

RECOVERY – OUR NUMBER ONE PRIORITY

Many people do not give their recovery priority. Although everyone wants to recover, there can seem a million more important things to be done first, usually for everyone else! Our recovery has to become the most important thing in our life. It needs to be our number one priority.

This can be very difficult for many of us, because we feel we are being selfish in putting our own needs first. But we need to ask ourselves, 'How can working towards our recovery be selfish?'

In the working-through process, especially at the beginning, we need our energy for ourselves. Part of the recovery process means accepting that we don't need to go along with what other people expect from us. We don't have to do or accept anything that we know is going to be detrimental to ourselves and our recovery. This is skilful. Our mental health depends upon nothing less!

THE FIRST LAYER

Recovery is not as simple as we would like it to be. In the beginning, it feels as though we are taking one step forward then two steps back. This is why so many people feel they are never going to recover. It is also part of the reason why so many people become discouraged and give up.

We need to understand the step-by-step process of working through the various stages of recovery. Understanding the working-through process is of the utmost importance, yet it is rarely given the importance it needs in some treatment options.

Patience

One of the first things we need to learn is patience. Everyone, naturally enough, wants recovery right now. Not tonight, not tomorrow, not next week, but this very second. All this does is create further stress, which keeps the whole cycle going. Whether we like it or not, we all need to learn patience with the working-through process and with ourselves. Learning to be patient is learning to be kind to ourselves. Being kind to ourselves means we are not putting ourselves under any further unnecessary stress. This is skilful action.

We need to direct our energy into the determination to commit ourselves, time and again, to the working-through process, despite setbacks. While the word 'setbacks' can appear to be negative, in reality they aren't. As we progress further down the path of recovery, we see they are our teachers – teaching us how to recover and teaching us to become our real self! I discuss setbacks in more detail in 'Understanding setbacks' below.

I speak about needing to bring our emotional development to the level of our intellectual development and this is what setbacks do. They demonstrate very clearly when we are holding our emotional development back. They teach us when we are not being responsible for ourselves, when we are invalidating ourselves by trying to be who we think we should be.

In the early stages of recovery we don't see this constructive aspect of our setbacks. In the beginning we see them as simply setbacks that are frustrating, frightening and what we think are signs that we won't ever recover. We will if we are totally committed and determined.

The working-through process

At first, the working-through process may seem to be difficult and confusing, and some people can feel daunted and overwhelmed by the amount of effort needed. It is worth it! Everything that is required from us during the working-through process will be given back to us in the sheer joy and total freedom that recovery brings. It is not just freedom from our anxiety disorder, it is also the freedom to be ourselves, not who we think we should be.

The working-through process is similar for everyone. The only difference is our personal threshold to stress. Some people may have reached the point where they cannot tolerate even the smallest amount of stress; others may have a higher threshold. The time it takes people to recover will vary. The individual threshold to stress is taken into account, but the amount of effort and discipline we put into our recovery is most important.

Our first panic attack or experience of high anxiety is usually triggered by either a build-up of stress or a major life stress. In other words, the anxiety and/or attack happened when we reached the limit of our individual threshold to stress. This doesn't mean we are weak. It simply means we have reached our limit to stress, just as most people will reach their limit to stress at one point or other in their life. Some people develop migraines; others develop high blood pressure. For people who have anxiety disorder, when the anxiety or attack is triggered, our continual worry about them increases our anxiety and in turn lowers our threshold to stress.

It is not so much the external stress which creates our difficulties. It is the way we perceive and deal with it that creates the problems. We deal with stress by trying to be who we think we should be. We turn off any emotions we may have, such as anger or grief, and take care of everyone else. So many people have commented to me that in times of a major stress they were fine. They were able to look after everyone else, do everything that needed to be done and they can't understand why they are now having problems. And that is the problem. They were not taking care of themselves!

As we begin the working-through process, it is helpful if we have an understanding of how low our threshold to stress is and how high our anxiety is. If our threshold to stress is now extremely low, we may not be able to tolerate even the smallest daily stress. Our threshold to stress would be zero while our anxiety level would be ten. At level five we would be able to tolerate the stress of daily life, but we will find our anxiety level rising if there is a break in our normal daily routine. At level ten we will be able to deal with almost any stress without becoming anxious.

The working-through process means working to increase our stress threshold back to normal levels while decreasing our anxiety level. Using the scale below will help us to estimate our levels.

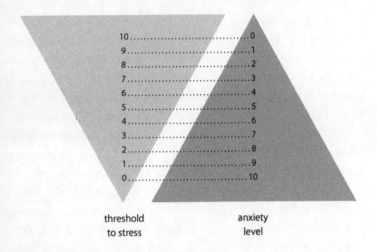

threshold   anxiety
to stress   level

It's of no use just hearing or reading about panic anxiety management skills. We have to practise them. There have been occasions when we say we're not getting any better, and nothing has changed. If we are not getting results it usually means we are not practising enough, or even not practising at all!

Understanding setbacks

Setbacks are unavoidable. In fact, the more setbacks we have, the better! Each setback teaches us more about ourselves and our disorder. They challenge us to strengthen and refine our cognitive skills, and challenge us to bring our emotional development to the level of our intellectual development.

To work through to recovery we need to understand why

setbacks happen. As an example, our threshold to stress may now be at level zero. At the lower threshold levels, we get caught up time and again in our panic- and anxiety-producing thoughts and symptoms. When we begin the process of recovery we need to meditate every day, and we need to become mindful and learn to control our thoughts. This is what is important at these levels. Learning to manage and control our disorder.

As we practise and begin to develop our skills, our threshold to stress moves to level one. We then experience our first break-through – we feel no fear or anxiety. This brings complete clarity of thought and a sense of total freedom. All fear of our panic and anxiety is lost and the sense of freedom can be exhilarating.

Our emotional understanding briefly integrates with that of our intellectual understanding. Our perception of our disorder changes. We see emotionally how it is all being created. If we dissociate we see and understand emotionally how it happens and how we get caught up in our panic and anxious thoughts about it. But any stress higher than level one will be enough to start the whole cycle again. Inevitably, this happens and we have a setback.

Again, it is not so much the stress itself that causes the setback, it is how we think and deal with the stress and how we think and deal with the re-emergence of our panic and anxiety symptoms.

When a stress is higher than our threshold, we automatically slip back to being 'who we think we should be' and we slip back into our anxiety disorder thinking. Anxiety and panic follow. We become so caught up in it all over again that we think the break-through was a fluke and that we are not going to recover.

When this happens we need to identify why we have had a setback. We need to become aware of the current stresses in our life and how we are reacting to them. Whatever the stress is, it will be higher than we can tolerate at this point. If we are working from zero tolerance to stress, identification of why we are having a setback is not difficult as the normal day-to-day stress will trigger our automatic cycle of thinking and behaving.

It could be that we dissociated and had an attack, and hooked into our panic and anxiety thoughts. We may have been thinking about a personal situation and how we can resolve it. We may have been thinking about how guilty we feel about something that we did or did not do or said or did not say. We may have said yes to doing something when we actually wanted to say no. We may have acted from the position of being who we thought we should be, and in doing so invalidated ourselves in some way. There may be family problems, a difficult financial or work situation, or children home on school holidays. Catching a virus and being physically sick. Any of these and more can trigger our panic- and anxiety-producing thoughts.

If we are not sure why we are having a setback, we can write down a list of everything that is currently happening in our life. To complete the list, we can write down how many times we have taken time out to meditate or practise some other form of relaxation. Then estimate how much time we have put into working with our thinking. That usually gives us the complete answer as to why we are having a setback.

When we become aware of why it has happened, the next step is to resolve any issues relating to the stress and to let the setback happen without buying into thoughts that we will never recover, or that we are hopeless and a failure. Our threshold to stress will continue to rise as long as we continue with our management skills. We then reach level two. Our emotional understanding again integrates with our intellectual understanding and the sense of clarity and freedom reappears. But any stress higher than level two will trigger a setback. Again we go through the principles outlined above. This is when we need to have patience. This is the working-through process.

When we have a setback, we need to become aware and ask the following questions:

- What was the current stress that triggered the setback?
- How did I think about it?
- How did I react to it?
- How did I deal with it?
- Did I deal with it in a realistic way, or in a way that added to my stress?
- Did I deal with it from my expectations and demands of how I think I should be?
- Am I still meditating? If not, why not?
- Am I still using mindfulness as a cognitive technique during the day? If not, why not?

If we are working from level zero, the first breakthrough usually only lasts for about an hour as the stress of daily life triggers our automatic way of thinking. With continued practice, our threshold to stress will continue to rise and we will begin to experience days and then weeks of clarity and freedom.

When we have a setback after these periods, everything seems much worse and more hopeless. It isn't. It is only the comparison between these two ways of being that makes it appear so. As long as we keep practising and working with it, we will ultimately be free of fears and of our disorder.

Acceptance revisited

Our levels of acceptance fluctuate during the working-through process. As we experience a setback, we get caught up in our old way of thinking and feeling. Some people may have renewed doubts that they have the disorder, and worry once again that the diagnosis may be incorrect. Non-acceptance means we are only making the situation worse for ourselves. We all have periods of doubt about the diagnosis. If this happens, it is important to discuss it with our doctor.

Compounding these doubts are the anxiety and panic attack symptoms and how they swap and change. Once we get on top of one symptom, another one takes its place. Any new symptom needs to be checked by our doctor, even though sometimes we may feel like we have hypochondria. However, it is more important for us to know what the new symptoms are instead of continually worrying. If we are told that the new symptom is another anxiety symptom, we need to accept the diagnosis and not get caught in the vicious circle again.

Even when we do accept that we are indeed experiencing an anxiety disorder, we place unrealistic expectations and demands on ourselves. A workshop participant was very upset during a workshop. He said to me:

'I should never have had that panic attack. It should never have happened; I am not scared of the shopping centre so it shouldn't have happened there. I can't believe that I have let myself down like this.'

Why 'shouldn't' it have happened? How did he let himself down? He had panic disorder. This means he will have an attack on occasions. Yet he was not accepting this reality, and in not doing so he added additional, unnecessary stress and anxiety to his situation.

THE SECOND LAYER

When we first begin to work on our recovery using mindfulness as a cognitive technique, we work with our obvious, 'loud', attention-getting panic anxiety thoughts and fears. As our mindfulness skills develop, we see the next layer of thoughts that also create our anxiety and panic.

One of the classic ways we create unnecessary stress is by thinking, 'What will people think?' What do you think when you hear a knock on the door?

'Oh no, I don't want anyone here. I haven't made the beds, vacuumed the house, washed the walls and curtains, cleaned the windows, done the dishes and steam-cleaned everything else since last night. I haven't any make-up on. My hair is a mess. What are they going to think? Oh no, here comes the anxiety. I can't breathe. What am I going to do now?'

We immediately generate anxiety by the way we are thinking. In reality, all that has happened is that someone has knocked on the door! We need to see how we can trigger our anxiety by the way we think about even the most ordinary everyday situations. We need to learn to deal with these situations and see them as they really are:

'Someone is at the door. The house is untidy. Okay, so the house isn't going to be a feature in a "beautiful homes of the year" magazine. I have no make-up on and my hair is a mess. They will just have to get over it. I will see what they want. If I don't want them to stay, I will tell them I am having a bad hair day and can they come back at a time that's suitable for both of us.'

Always remember, our mental health needs to be more important than what other people think of us.

Another classic example is how we take responsibility for other people's problems. How many hours have you spent on the phone, allowing people to download all their problems onto you? And they usually always ring at dinner time. Have you noticed that? How many hours have you spent giving the most excellent advice that no one takes, while your dinner goes cold? All because we are too frightened to tell them, 'This is not a good time,' in case they think badly of us.

If that isn't enough, how do you feel once you get off the phone? Do you think:

'Poor Jane, she has so many problems. I feel so bad for her. I am so worried about her. There has to be something more I can do for her. What if that happened to me? What would I do? Oh no, what if that does happen to me? What if it did? I can't think about it. I have to stop thinking about it. But what if it did? Why is my heart racing? Oh no, what's my pulse? Oh, it is so high!'

Then a week later Jane rings back at her normal time, your dinner time, and downloads the same problems as last week. But this time with the added bonus of the latest weekly update, which adds another 30 minutes to the phone call. And, of course, she hasn't taken any of the advice you have given her over the last few weeks. There are always numerous reasons why she hasn't, and they all sound very legitimate. All the same, she asks you what can she do, and pleads with you to help her.

This time your annoyance begins to surface, and you think: 'Why does she always ring me? Doesn't she feed her family? Why can't she work it out herself? I am so sick of this. How can I be so mean? Oh no, now I can't breathe, I feel dizzy, here is comes again.'

A far less stressful and compassionate approach would be:

'Jane, I am serving dinner so I am not able to spend time with you at the moment. I realise you're distressed, but we have discussed this a number of times. I need you to be able to see what you can do to help yourself in this situation. All I am doing for you each week is contributing to your overall problem, because nothing is changing. Can you think about this? See what you can do and find out who you can contact for further assistance. We can speak at another time.'

Don't let this become yet another stressful situation by worrying and feeling guilty: 'What will she think of me? Why did I do that? She needs help. Why was I so selfish? Oh no, my heart is racing, I feel shaky, but I have to get dinner. I feel too sick to eat.'

We need to see how our need to be all things to all people plays a significant role in creating unnecessary stress, and how this can induce setbacks.

COMMUNICATE, COMMUNICATE, COMMUNICATE

As we recover, we begin to change. And as much as everyone wants us to recover, this can be frightening for our partner and family members. It is so important that everyone discusses this. Not just on a superficial level, but in depth. We need to be able to talk about any fears we may have as a result of this process, and so too do our partner and family members. They need to talk about any fears they may have as a result of the changes we are making. I can't emphasise enough how important this is. If we are able to be open and honest with each other, our relationships can strengthen and deepen. Communication is the key!

Avoidance behaviour: working it

Part of the process of recovery means working on our avoidance behaviour. Many people think that they need to approach their avoidance behaviour in a non-anxiety, non-panic state. It doesn't work like this. We need to be anxious, and a panic attack or two while working on our avoidance behaviour would also be of benefit! Without them, we have nothing to practise on!

Recovery means we can be in any situation or place, and if we become anxious or have an attack we can control it then and there, without needing to leave and without even thinking we need to leave.

Most of us use a graded exposure technique when working on our avoidance behaviour. As the name suggests, this means gradually exposing ourselves to the situations and places we have been avoiding. Although people find these techniques frightening, they are not as demanding as a 'flooding' technique, which involves exposing ourselves immediately to our most feared situations. These techniques can be counterproductive for some people.

When we first begin to do work on our avoidance behaviour using a graded exposure method, we need to remember that our mindfulness skills are usually very rudimentary and that it can be difficult for us to achieve all we want to achieve in a particular session. Some graded exposure programs ask that people stay in the situation or place until their panic and anxiety levels subside. In the early stages of recovery, this can be very difficult.

While our attack will subside in time, our anxiety can remain high because we attach to our thoughts: 'I can't do this. My anxiety is too high. What can I do? I feel terrible. Why hasn't the anxiety gone away? I hate this. What is wrong with me? Why can't I do this? I am such a failure. I am so weak. I should be able to do this.'

All these thoughts do is keep our anxiety going. Sometimes it is of greater benefit to simply go home, rather than fighting to stay and fighting to get our anxiety level down. Fighting it will only keep it going!

Going home is not defeat. It is not failure, as long as we go back out the next day and attempt it again. When we get home we can review where we became caught up. We can track back and see where and how we attached to our thoughts and how this created our anxiety and perhaps panic. Conducting a review like this will teach us more about our thoughts and symptoms, and show us where we need to become more mindful.

We can then 'begin again'. These two words can give us the freedom to let go of the times when our graded exposure program or practise of mindfulness did not work out the way we would have liked. All we need do is review where we can improve and then begin again. And we will be 'beginning again' quite a bit during the recovery process!

We also need to make allowances in working with a graded exposure program. We need the freedom to be able to do what feels right for us. And that does not necessarily mean 'I am out of here!' It means making allowances for ourselves.

We need to be able to set our own exposure program and we need to be able to control it. In some cases our program is set by other people, and we follow along doing what we think we should do. We feel the pressure to 'perform' as perfectly as possible to ensure we have 'the perfect recovery'.

All this does is make us resistant to doing the exposure program. We need to have a choice, and we need the flexibility to be able to choose what we want to do at any point in the program. If we know we have a choice, we can take back the power!

Seeing the choices

If we want to have a mobile phone with us when we are practising our exposure program, then we carry one. If we know we can call for assistance at any time, this eases the pressure. If we need to sit behind a potted palm when we first visit a restaurant again, then we sit behind the potted palm. If we need to sit in an aisle seat next to the exit in the theatre or cinema, then we sit in an aisle seat next to the exit. If we need the security of a tranquilliser in our wallet, then we need the security of a tranquilliser in our wallet. When we can approach our exposure work in a more relaxed way, we will be able to accomplish so much more than if we have a list of should and should nots in our head.

Another allowance is breaking down the time we know we will have to spend in any given situation. It may be a business meeting, an evening with friends or doing the shopping. It could be anything. If we know something will take two hours, work with the first hour first. Don't even think about the second hour. If it is too difficult and our anxiety level doesn't settle down, we can leave after the first hour. Usually by the second hour we are not even aware that the first hour is over, because we have become involved with what we are doing instead of the anxiety and attacks.

Part of our exposure program may be doing the shopping

alone. This can be broken down into easier steps. To begin with, we can go to the shop early in the morning. We will feel more comfortable in letting the anxiety and attack happen if the shop is not too crowded. As we become more confident in letting it happen, we can begin to shop at different times of the day.

In the beginning there may be times when we feel we will have to leave a situation. If it becomes too difficult to manage, then leave, not with a sense of failure but accepting that this time it was too difficult. A sense of failure defeats us, not only in the short term but also in the long term. Accept it and let go of the worrying. There will be other times when we will be able to do it as long as we keep practising.

Making allowances is not giving in; it is working with the disorder. Doing nothing is giving in. In the early stages of recovery, making allowances helps us to reduce the amount of pressure we feel. Making allowances indefinitely means we are not putting ourselves under enough pressure!

Sometimes the question arises about how much we need to practise working on our avoidance behaviour. Initially, having to confront various situations and places we have avoided places us under more stress. We need to learn to walk a fine line. There are going to be times when we feel we want to give up and we begin to despair of ever recovering. There may be times when we feel this way, but we continually push ourselves without being aware of how much more anxiety is being generated. Then we give up through exhaustion and despair.

Working with our avoidance behaviour and the whole process of recovery means we need to learn to care for ourselves. We need to learn when it is appropriate to pull back and take a break, as long as the break doesn't go on for weeks. After the break, begin again.

Practising mindfulness

We need to be mindful of our anticipatory anxiety. We can set ourselves up for further anxiety and panic hours or days before we do any graded exposure work. We need to be mindful and work with these thoughts before we leave home! It can save us additional panic and anxiety while we are working on our exposure program.

The more mindful we become, the more we work with our thoughts, the easier it becomes to break through our avoidance behaviour. And the more we work with our thoughts, the more our perception of our attacks and anxiety changes. Once this happens, it becomes easier to work through to recovery.

Have you ever tried to have a panic attack? Have you ever tried to deliberately make yourself anxious, make yourself panic? Try it and see what happens!

Medication

Part of our recovery may mean a gradual withdrawal from our medication, including tranquillisers or antidepressants. We need to do this under medical supervision, and our doctor will prepare a reduction plan for us which we will need to follow.

During this phase of my own recovery, I found that my daily practice of meditation and my mindfulness skills enabled me to work through my withdrawal symptoms in the same way I had worked through my attacks and anxiety. I let the withdrawal symptoms happen and did not become involved with my anxious thoughts about them!

Alcohol dependence

If we have a dependency on alcohol, we need to address this as part of our recovery. Organisations such as Alcoholics Anonymous can be of assistance and benefit, and can provide the support we need. Again our panic anxiety management skills can be utilised during this period.

What issues do you need to address during the recovery process?

- Avoidance behaviour
- Prescribed drug addiction
- Alcohol dependency
- Past personal issues
- Current personal issues
- Childhood abuse issues

Taking care of ourselves

A proper diet and getting enough sleep are very important in helping to raise our threshold to stress. If we have eating problems, it is important we seek advice to help re-establish normal eating patterns. If we are having difficulty sleeping, we can use our meditation technique to assist us in going to sleep at night or going back to sleep if we have woken with an attack. Instead of actually meditating, we simply let the meditation technique take us into sleep.

Exercise also plays an important part in the recovery process, and establishing a regular exercise program can be beneficial. Although many of us feel totally exhausted as a result of our ongoing struggle with panic and anxiety, exercise helps us to break through this fatigue. This sounds like a contradiction, but in reality it isn't. The more exercise we do, the less fatigue we will feel.

Relearning

The working-through process also involves relearning what it is like to be 'normal'. We lose sight of what it is like to be 'normal', and it is not unusual for people to interpret 'normalcy' as a setback! It isn't, we just have to relearn.

This means relearning to have a 'normal' bad day without reacting with fear that 'it is all coming back'. Returning to 'normal' means we will have bad days just like everyone else.

We will probably have days when we feel unwell. It doesn't mean a return of the disorder – it means we are feeling unwell. We need to make sure we are eating properly and getting enough sleep. If not, we will feel tired and irritable just like everyone does when they neglect themselves. Recovery is a learning process, learning to manage and control our anxiety disorder and learning about ourselves.

Use the following check list when you are having a setback to help you isolate the reasons why it has happened and what you can do to assist yourself in working through it.

SETBACK CHECK LIST

☐ Are you learning to be kind to yourself?

☐ Do you accept the diagnosis of an anxiety disorder?

☐ Are you being completely honest with your doctor?

☐ Are you asking for assistance when you need it?

☐ If you are using medication, are you following the guidelines prescribed by your doctor?

☐ Do you blame or mentally abuse yourself because you have an anxiety disorder or because you have had a setback?

☐ Is your recovery your number one priority?

☐ Are you trying to have the perfect recovery?

☐ Are you learning and understanding all you need to know about panic attacks and anxiety?

☐ Do you ensure you are taking at least twenty minutes a day to meditate or use another relaxation technique?

☐ Are you developing mindfulness skills?

☐ Are you committed and disciplined in practising this daily or only on occasions when you think about it?

☐ Are you facing situations and places that you have avoided while you develop mindfulness skills?

☐ Can you identify the stress that created the setback?

☐ How did you think about it?

☐ How did you react to it?

☐ How did you deal with it?

☐ Did you deal with it in a realistic way?

☐ Did you deal with it from your expectations and demands of how you think you should be?

GOALS

I tell people to be careful when setting goals. They can be restrictive because of our need to be perfect, which means we need to reach our goals perfectly! And setting goals means we 'have to' reach them, no matter what. This can mean we resist straight away!

I say to everyone just have one goal. Recovery. This takes the pressure away in trying to meet 'goal one through to goal 101'. And it allows us the freedom to be spontaneous and creative during recovery.

The more aware we become, the more we will feel our own intuition coming through. So many people tell me that they feel their intuition prompting them to go further into recovery, or to push past their limits of their avoidance behaviour, but they don't act on it. Why? It's us teaching us, showing us, how to recover.

If we can begin to act on our intuition at any point of the recovery process, it will enable us to move through to recovery more easily and more creatively. This is why I say don't set goals, because if we begin to follow our intuition we can go from 'goal twenty-five to goal fifty-nine' in one swift move. Or we may realise that the goals we have set are too restrictive or unnecessary, and so we can drop them altogether and change the direction of our recovery entirely. We need to listen to ourselves.

CHAPTER 14

The need to belong

In the Tibetan Buddhist Shambhala teachings, 'the definition of bravery is not being afraid of our self' (Trungpa, 1986). We are frightened of ourselves and our fear is multilayered. At the top level is our anxiety disorder and beneath it is the fear of our self.

The first stage of recovery is learning to reduce our anxiety levels using either meditation or another relaxation technique and developing our mindfulness cognitive skills. We become aware of our 'loud' panic- and anxiety-producing thoughts, and we see how they create our symptoms. We learn to see that we have a choice in either becoming involved with them or in letting them go.

As our mindfulness skills increase, we see not only the 'loud' panic- and anxiety-producing thoughts, we become aware of other thoughts. These thoughts show us how they too can activate our anxiety in ordinary everyday situations. As our mindfulness skills develop further, we see that these thoughts show us how our need for approval permeates our life.

A PERSONAL CHOICE

We need to become aware of these thoughts and their associated feelings. We will see how our anxiety and panic can increase when we are not respecting and accepting ourselves, or being responsible for ourselves.

When we say yes and we mean no, we see how our anxiety and feelings of panic can increase. They can increase when we take responsibility for everyone's feelings, and when we go out of our way to make everyone feel happy. We will see how our fear of hurting or upsetting people in the slightest way increases our anxiety.

We will see how we are constantly feeling guilty. We will also see our perfectionist behaviour and how this impacts on everything that we do, and how this generates anxiety and panic.

When we can see this it creates confusion because what can we do? We can let these thoughts go, but we think we are in a no-win situation. We think there is nothing we can do about our overall circumstances, and we feel trapped.

When we are aware of this, we can choose to continue as we have been doing or we can choose to become responsible for ourselves. This means saying no when we *mean no*, and it means *not* taking responsibility for other people's feelings. Self-responsibility also means understanding why we *do not* need to feel guilty all of the time, and it means *not* trying to be perfect. It means allowing ourselves to feel the full depth of our emotions.

In doing so, we allow our emotional development to unfold and we develop a more authentic, real sense of self and identity. We belong to ourselves rather than 'needing to belong'. Taking this step can generate further fears:

- People will think I am selfish

- This is not caring for others
- People will think I am egotistical
- I can't do this
- I won't be able to do this
- This is too hard
- I'm scared I'll fail
- What if I do fail?
- I'd rather not try in the first place because I couldn't bear it if I failed
- People will think I am stupid
- What if I do succeed, what will happen to me? I'll be different from everyone else.

Can you see the central theme in these fears? They come back to a core fear: 'What will people think of me?'

THE THIRD LAYER

I have spoken about the first and second layers of recovery in Chapter 13. In the workshops I run, I've found it is helpful to put the third layer of recovery into a specific framework. This way we can see and understand where we are, and where skilful action can take us. As a starting point, I draw upon the work of Abraham Maslow and Ken Wilber.

Abraham Maslow is credited as being the pioneer in humanist and existential psychology, and Ken Wilber is a leading theorist in the study of human consciousness. Maslow developed a hierarchy of 'self needs', which demonstrates our potential development throughout life (Maslow, 1954). This hierarchy can be our guide to understanding where we are and how we can develop further emotionally.

MASLOW'S HIERARCHY OF NEEDS

6. Self-transcendence
5. Self-actualisation
4. Self-esteem needs
3. The need to belong
2. Safety needs
1. Survival needs

Development in these terms means that we need to be able to meet the set of needs at each level of the hierarchy or 'ladder' before we can develop further. Ken Wilber, who writes extensively on this subject, proposes an overall model of development based upon a spectrum of consciousness. In other words, based upon a greater expansion of personal awareness. That is, as we move through each level of development, 'each set of needs . . . the self will eventually grow beyond these views and expand its awareness' (Wilber, K., 1996). The operative word is 'expand'. The more aware we become, the more our perception of ourself unfolds. In doing so, as Wilber states, we 'step off the present rung, dis-identify with it, and then identify with the next higher rung'.

The first set of needs in Maslow's hierarchy are our physiological (survival) needs. We need air to breathe and nourishment and obviously these needs have been met. As they have been met the next set of needs comes into play and these are our safety needs, both personal and environmental. For most of us, these basic needs have been met, although people who were abused as children may still have personal safety issues that need to be resolved. At this level we may be at an impasse as adults, and find ourselves in relationships where the abuse from childhood is carried over into our adult relationships. If this is the case, being able to meet our personal safety needs becomes part of the work we need to do.

The next set of needs is the 'need to belong'. We need to belong to our families, our peer group and society as a whole. We need to be liked and loved. And this is where we all 'live'. We are still trying to find a sense of belonging. Our way of trying to meet this set of needs means we have given away any sense of personal self, any sense of personal power as we try to meet the expectations of who we think we should be. If we can become who we think we should be, people will think well of us, and if they do think well of us, then we can belong.

At this level in the hierarchy, we feel there is no room for us to move in order to address the self-esteem needs. The self-esteem needs demand much from us, and they are in direct opposition to the need to belong. The table below outlines the differences between these two ways of being.

From our vantage point within the hierarchy, the demands of self-esteem are frightening to contemplate. This brings in all our fears of not being likable, of not being lovable, of not belonging. It also calls into question our 'rules' about who we should be, about compassion and what selfishness really means. From this level on the 'ladder', our awareness does not enable us to see the 'bigger picture'.

Need to belong	Assumption/ outcome	Self-esteem – skilful action
I often say yes when I mean no	I have no choice	I say no when I mean no
If I say no to people, I am being selfish	I have no right to put my needs first	I am honest with myself and others
If I say no to people, they will be hurt	I hurt myself instead by saying yes	I am responsible for myself
If I say no to people, I feel guilty	Guilt confirms my worst fears about myself	I treat myself with respect
If I say no to people, they may not like me	I reject myself	I honour myself
When I say yes to people, I feel resentful	Why does it always have to be me?	I am responsible for my feelings
When I say yes to people, I feel used	I feel angry at myself and them	I am responsible for my choices
When I say yes to people, I feel stressed	I should be able to handle it	I am not creating unnecessary stress for myself
When I say yes to people, I smile	I don't want people to feel it is an imposition	If it is an imposition, I say no
I can always see different points of view	I am unsure which view to take	I respect my own opinions
I can't make a decision	I know what I want, but is it the same as what others want?	I trust my own opinions

I go out of my way to ensure everyone is happy	Isn't this what I am supposed to do?	I am only responsible for my own happiness
I always try to be perfect in everything I do	Is there any other way?	I honour myself and my abilities
I help people all the time, but when I need it, they don't have time to help me	I feel confused and rejected	I have realistic expectations of myself and others
I never express my anger, even when people have used me or abused my trust	I turn my anger on myself	I've learnt about anger's hidden message about my perceptions and expectations of myself and other people
I don't cry	I should be able to handle anything	I feel and express my emotions
If I do cry I feel stupid	It shows that I am weak	Expressing my emotions is healthy
I always help others at work even though it puts me way behind	People expect this from me	I am responsible for my time management
I feel so ashamed when people criticise me	I try to be as perfect as I can	I am able to look at the validity of the criticism, taking it on board if applicable or setting a boundary
I cannot spend time just sitting, reading or relaxing	There is always too much to do	I take time to relax and enjoy quiet time with myself

Need to belong	Assumption/ outcome	Self-esteem – skilful action
I can't spend time alone	It makes me feel nervous for some reason	I am comfortable in my own company
My needs and wants don't count	Do I have any?	I am aware of my needs and wants, and meet them
I always do what everyone wants	Isn't this what I am supposed to do?	I say no when I want to
I can't say what I want to do	Everyone will think it is stupid	I can be assertive
I can't speak up at meetings	I do not want to look like an idiot	I can express myself with dignity
I have ideas but don't say anything, and when someone else has the same idea and puts it forward it is always accepted without question	This always amazes me. They aren't treated as idiots	I respect my ideas and express them without fear
I can't ask questions	People will think I am stupid	I know that asking questions is how we learn
I do not have a choice in anything I do	There is a choice?	There is always a choice
I can't speak in public	I will make a fool of myself	Why will I? I value my opinions and knowledge

I feel so different from everyone else	I try so hard to be like everyone else	I am myself and I honour the differences
I can't bear people around me being angry or annoyed	I think it is my fault	I separate myself psychologically from other people
I don't believe my partner when they say they love me	I don't like myself, I loathe myself, I hate myself	I accept and take responsibility for myself with care and respect
I do not believe people if they say they like me	How can they?	It is my responsibility to accept who I am
I can't identify my feelings	I shouldn't have feelings	I identify, accept and allow myself to feel my own feelings
I feel smothered by other people	I shouldn't feel like this	I set a boundary
I am the peacekeeper in the family	It is my responsibility	Not taking care of other people's problems
If I am told I am doing a good job at work, I don't believe it	I worry that people will find out that I'm a fraud	I acknowledge and take responsibility for my skills and abilities
I try never to make mistakes	So people won't know I am hopeless	I learn from my mistakes
I have never thought of myself as intelligent	I am stupid, hopeless, dumb	This isn't intelligent thinking
I can't understand why I have an anxiety disorder		I can

Self-esteem demands a different way of looking at ourselves and the world around us. At this level, it is not so much the need to belong, or the need to be liked or loved by everyone; it is the need to belong to ourselves.

If we are unable to meet our self-esteem needs, it is going to be difficult for us to reach our full potential at the self-actualisation level. At the moment, all our energy is being used to keep us where we think we should be, not where we could be. We have so little to give to meet our potential, because our need to belong sabotages any attempts we make to realise this level. After all, what will people think?

The last set of needs on Maslow's hierarchy is the need for self-transcendence. This means going beyond the personal sense of self and beginning to identify with the spiritual self. But that is another book entirely!

Anxiety as our teacher

The more aware we become, the more we will see how our daily interactions with other people create so much of our anxiety. This is when our anxiety can become our teacher if we allow it to. We will see how we do not accept ourselves, our needs and our wants. We will see how we are violating our responsibility to ourselves and how this generates our feelings of worthlessness and helplessness. We will see that we have a choice in being who we think we should be, or becoming all that we could be.

Guilt

Guilt is a passive emotion and comes with the 'package' of being all things to all people. It is a by-product of our lack of acceptance of ourselves and our own needs. And this is why we can have difficulty knowing exactly what our needs are.

We can feel guilty about anything. We have a conversation with someone, and then review the conversation in our mind. We worry about the inflection in our voice, in case the person has taken what we said in the 'wrong' way. We worry about our facial expression in case other people 'read' something into it that wasn't there. We worry that we should be doing this, or shouldn't have done that. We feel guilty if we don't meet our expectations of who we think we should be, if we are not meeting other people's expectations of us.

CASE HISTORY

Marg

Marg put the phone down, sighing with annoyance. She felt her anxiety begin to rise. Her friend had wanted her to look after her children this coming Saturday afternoon. 'If it is convenient,' her friend had said. It wasn't. Marg had wanted this Saturday as a day for herself because her husband was taking their children to a sports carnival. 'You know I don't like to impose, Marg, but it would mean so much for me to have a few hours to catch up with some friends.'

Marg took a deep breath. She wanted to say no, but now she felt guilty. She knew her friend was like herself, insofar as neither of them had any free time for themselves. In saying no to her friend she thought she was being selfish and she felt her guilt increase. 'You understand, don't you, Marg? This would be so good for me. What do you think?'

'Of course I will,' Marg said as her guilt disappeared, and was replaced with resentment and increasing anxiety.

Does this sound familiar? It can become quite complex, because every time we turn around there is someone else's feelings to consider or that we think we have to consider. Where are our own needs in this? They have taken a 'back seat'. Even if we do meet our own needs, any sense of respecting ourselves is gone. We are too busy beating ourselves up, thinking we are selfish, horrible or disgusting. Is it any wonder we feel anxious?

But we can actually use our anxiety and guilt in a constructive way. We can learn from these feelings, and we can ultimately defeat them by seeing where we are not accepting and being responsible for ourselves. When we can see this, we are then able to become more skilful in our thoughts and actions towards ourselves and other people.

Boundaries

Part of skilful action is learning where to set boundaries. A boundary can be either physical or psychological, or both, and is used to define who we are. Setting and keeping our boundaries protects us from our own and other people's expectations of who we should be.

As an example, when we are standing in a queue and someone comes and stands right next to us, we feel they are invading our 'space' so we take a step away from them to protect that space. When we do this, we are setting a physical boundary. If we are in a physically abusive relationship, we need to set physical boundaries to protect ourselves from being abused. And this may mean that we leave the abusive situation permanently.

Psychologically, we take on board whatever anyone says to us. We don't examine it to see if what is being said is true for us. Even if we don't think it is true, we take it on board and adjust our perceptions and behaviour to suit.

Setting a psychological boundary means that we don't take everything on board. We examine it, and if it is not valid or true for us we don't become involved with it or go along with it to placate others. In this way we define ourselves, our perceptions and opinions by separating ourselves from other people's perceptions and opinions.

It can be difficult and frightening to set boundaries because we have been taught that compassion means taking care of everyone's feelings and meeting their wants and needs. This is what most of us think compassion means. But it doesn't! Compassion is no harm to self or others.

We need to see how we harm ourselves by getting caught up in feeling guilty, by being the perfectionist, by trying to make everyone happy and by becoming anxious as a result. Saying no to someone is not harming them. It is being honest, and honesty is the foundation of a healthy relationship.

We don't see the harm we do to ourselves, and other people, from our perspective at the 'need to belong' level of Maslow's hierarchy of needs. We aren't seeing the 'bigger picture'. When we are responsible for other people, we don't give *them* the opportunity to see and examine the reasons for their own expectations, annoyances, anger, frustration and all their other feelings that can cause them pain and suffering. People may not want to take responsibility for themselves, but this is *their* choice. It doesn't mean that we need to step in and do it for them.

In some instances, skilful compassionate action means standing back. Sometimes our actions in being responsible for other people, in trying to 'rescue' them, unknowingly contribute to their situation or circumstances in unskilful ways.

With psychological boundaries in place, we will not become caught up in feeling horrible, selfish, guilty or anxious when we stop being all things to all people. We will be able to see the situation exactly how it is. With boundaries in place, we will be able to separate ourselves and not become caught up in the never-ending cycle of guilt and anxiety.

Expectations

Whether we are aware of it or not, we all have a sense of 'pride' in the expectations we have of ourselves, however unrealistic they may be. And when we can't meet these expectations, we beat ourselves up about it. We expect ourselves to be perfect in all that we do, and when we fall short, we become anxious. And while we are doing this, we are discounting the reality of our own experience by discounting our intelligence, our skills, our talents and individual qualities and our interactions with others.

We may receive a job promotion, graduate from university with distinction, succeed in our chosen field, excel in any area of our life, yet we disregard these accomplishments. We certainly don't take pride in them. They 'don't really count'. We think they must be some sort of 'fluke' or error. We can live in fear for years with the thought, 'What if people find out I am not as good as they think I am?'

We can be extremely creative and can offer much to ourselves, family, friends and employers with our creative ideas or strategies. Yet we don't voice our ideas, because we are frightened that people will think we are stupid or silly. How many times have we come up with an idea or strategy and held it back? Then we find someone else comes up with a similar idea a few months later, and it is accepted and sometimes applauded for its originality and viability. All the while we beat ourselves up because we cannot meet the expectations we have of ourselves!

CASE HISTORY

Janet

Janet looked at her friend. 'Do you know,' she said,' most of my early life I spent trying to please my parents. I was always criti-cised and never felt I was good enough. Later, I always thought everything I did had to be perfect, the perfect wife, mother, cook, dressmaker.

'One of the things that helped me when I started to take control of my panic disorder and agoraphobia was to take time out each day to look at the things I could do well, and not always be busting myself to do better. Also learning to accept praise and learning to have an opinion on things, even if I kept it to myself. I used to be proud of my perfectionism, now I hate what it has done to me. I still have to ask myself some-times when I see the perfectionist tendency arise, "Does it really matter?"'

Not accepting ourselves is not skilful or compassionate and is a major violation of ourselves. Until we can accept ourselves as we are right now, we will be in continual conflict because we are trying to be someone other than who we are. And this generates anxiety and depression.

It also impacts on our lives in other ways. When we don't accept ourselves, we are unable to accept other people as they are. Although we may not be aware of it, we keep on trying to 'change' ourselves to fit the image of who we think we should be, and we keep trying to change other people to fit the image of who we want them to be. Other people can also do this to themselves and to us. This creates a great deal of underlying tension and conflict within our relationships.

We long for the 'happy ever after' with our partner, family members and friends. We think to ourselves, 'If I just try a bit harder and if they just try a bit harder' to be who we want them to be, all our private and secret yearnings will be realised.

Part of our lack of acceptance of ourselves means we do not acknowledge, let alone accept, our intelligence, our skills and our creativity. We think we are stupid, we think we have to keep on trying to 'prove' ourselves and we worry that we will be exposed as a fraud. We *are* intelligent, we *do* have a great number of skills, we just don't recognise them!

So many people say to me, 'But what if people find out what I am really like?' What if *we find* out what we are really like? What if we *find* out that we are intelligent? That we do indeed have many skills? And what if people do appreciate us for who we are, not who we think we should be. What then?

When we stop trying to be perfect, we take away so much of the pressure we place on ourselves, and we also find that we do not fail. In fact, we have much more energy to work more efficiently and productively, because we are not creating unnecessary stress or feeling guilty about 'what a terrible job we did'!

Our anxiety can become our teacher by showing us how we are violating and harming ourselves. When our anxiety points out the areas where we are doing this, we need to examine and question our beliefs about ourselves and who we think we should be. We need to see whether our beliefs are relevant and necessary to us now, or whether they are a carryover from the past. If we decide these beliefs are no longer necessary to us, we can then choose to live our life in a different, more skilful way.

Growth anxiety

Choosing to live our life more skilfully means we allow our emotional development to unfold. In doing so we 'dis-identify' with the 'need to belong' level and begin to work towards meeting our self-esteem needs. This means accepting ourselves, and taking responsibility for ourselves. It means honouring our own needs and taking care of ourselves by setting boundaries where we need to.

We may feel anxious as we begin to do this, but this anxiety is different. It is not 'anxiety disorder' anxiety; rather, it is 'growth' anxiety. We are taking the first steps in becoming ourselves and it is natural and normal for us to feel this way. If we can allow the 'growth' anxiety to be there, and not contaminate it with thoughts of 'What will people think?', we will then be able to move forward.

The more we practise skilful compassionate action, the more we see its simplicity, and in that simplicity is power and freedom. When we accept ourselves, we accept other people for who they are. When we take responsibility for our lives, we give back the responsibility to other people for their lives. We can then contribute to other people and society in much more healthier ways than we are able to now. The major contribution we can make in our lives, in the lives of other people and within society, is for us simply to be ourselves.

CHAPTER 15

Unmasked

PSYCHOTHERAPY

As we have seen, most of us learned as children that the expression of our emotions – anger, grief, sadness – was inappropriate. We thought that people wouldn't like us or love us if we expressed these emotions and so we suppressed them. Anger and sadness are primary emotions, and although they are suppressed they don't just 'go away'; they are still there. When situations in our daily life are similar to the ones we experienced as children, they can trigger our suppressed anger or sadness. Sometimes we may feel the anger or sadness before we suppress them; at other times we may suppress them straight away. We can then feel anxious or depressed and wonder why.

This is why it is important that we talk about our feelings, express them and work with them with the support of a therapist. We need to be totally open and honest with ourselves and our therapists. Letting ourselves work through this and allowing ourselves to feel our emotions is skilful and compassionate.

Psychotherapy or counselling isn't going to help us learn to manage and control our panic- and anxiety-producing thoughts.

They are not going to get us out of the house, into the supermarket or being able to drive again, or help us work through other forms of avoidance behaviour. This is what mindfulness or other cognitive behavioural techniques do.

From my experience, people who go into therapy after developing these skills go through to full recovery and stay recovered. Of course, not everyone is going to want to do this, and this is part of what recovery is all about. Recognising and doing what we need to do for ourselves.

Mindfulness or other cognitive strategies are targeted to our immediate situation, and teach us how to control and manage our panic and anxiety. But unlike other cognitive strategies, working with meditation and a mindfulness cognitive technique can show us current or past personal issues that we need to address, and psychotherapy can assist us with this. In fact, 'meditation may facilitate the psychotherapeutic process' (Taskforce on Meditation, 1977).

Psychotherapy is a two-way partnership between ourselves and our therapist. I see therapy working at two different levels. The first level is working with our knowledge of our childhood experiences. It looks at what happened to us as children. This may mean confronting our hurt, pain, anger, rage, grief and sadness, and learning not to become frightened of the power and intensity of these feelings. This is why it is so important for us to have a good working relationship with our therapist.

As we work with this, the second level of therapy comes into play, which involves issues of trust. I will return to this in a moment. At the first level, it is our responsibility when we are in therapy to work through our emotions, and not suppress them, run from them or deny them. It is also our responsibility to work all the way through, and not give up partway, otherwise we can remain a victim of our past and present and nothing much changes in the future.

Therapy can be difficult, but it is all part of the process and it is worth it! Sometimes we may feel anxious and panicky. Our anxiety and panic can teach us to understand why we are feeling this way. We may be resisting something that we don't want to face or deal with. We may break through and begin to see things as they really are. We could be getting in touch with our primary emotions and because they are so strong, we become frightened.

These are the types of issues that our therapist can help us work through, because all of the above brings up the second and much more subtle part of therapy. This second level deals not with what happened to us, but what we needed to do as children to feel loved and cared for. The second level of therapy applies to all of us, whether we come from an abusive background or not. We all adopted beliefs about ourselves and made decisions about who we should be based on these beliefs.

There is nothing wrong with this, but we have taken it to the extent that these beliefs, and our decisions based on them, are keeping us trapped emotionally in the past. We don't realise how these beliefs and decisions impact on us right now, in every aspect of our life, and how they create much of our underlying anxiety and depression. Our beliefs have meant that we unwittingly betrayed the trust and respect we could have developed in ourselves.

This is the reason why we may know intellectually that our anxiety and panic won't hurt us, but why we can't feel the truth of this emotionally. We don't trust ourselves or our intelligence.

As we peel back the 'onion', mindfulness will also show us how we are violating our responsibility to ourselves and that we do indeed have a choice in how we live our life. We can choose whether to change our beliefs or remain with the old ones. If we choose to change, we do so by skilful action – accepting ourselves as we are and being responsible for ourselves.

This is why therapy can be important: it helps us to get in touch, not just with our own emotions but, at the second level, with what we have unwittingly done to ourselves. Our therapist can assist us in seeing the choice, and supporting us, as we begin to take responsibility for our lives and change our beliefs to healthier and more mature ones. Part of this means learning to trust ourselves and learning to trust our therapist.

We need a therapist who is nonjudgmental. This enables us to learn to express our emotions and to change our beliefs in a non-judgmental and safe environment. If we decide to see a therapist, we need to choose our therapist carefully. We are not going to get anywhere if we have a therapist who:

- Just sits there and stares, rarely saying anything
- Nods off to sleep during the session
- Holds the floor, talking of their life experience or what they did on the weekend.

If this happens, and unfortunately it can, we need to find another therapist. Some people will stay in a therapy situation like this because of misguided loyalty to the therapist. We think, 'They must be tired,' or 'They just needed someone to talk to!'

They may be tired, they may just want to talk to someone, but why are we paying for it? And we pay for it in more ways than one. We need to take responsibility for ourselves and terminate therapy with them. If not, all we are doing is taking responsibility for the therapist and their needs. And we certainly won't recover this way!

If we have a therapist who helps us gain insight into our various issues but does nothing to support us to bring those insights into everyday living, then again we are not going to get very far either. All we will have is plenty of insights, and probably even more confused feelings. 'I understand, I realise it all now, but what can I do? Nothing has changed, so what is the point?'

It is our responsibility to work with our insights and change our perception and behaviour accordingly, and this can be done with assistance from our therapist. Sitting and talking, going round in circles about the same issues for years is not productive or healthy.

We may have a therapist who challenges us to bring our insights into everyday living, but we need to be responsible for ourselves and meet this challenge. If not, nothing much will change.

Other people will say to me, 'There is no point in being angry about my past. My therapist tells me I need to forgive everyone so I am trying to. But it doesn't take my panic, anxiety or my depression away'.

Nor will it if we go straight from insight to forgiveness. Forgiveness is a four-step process:
1. Knowledge and insight
2. Anger and grief
3. Acceptance
4. Possible forgiveness

I say 'possible', because some people, depending on individual circumstances or trauma, will find total forgiveness difficult. Trying to forgive is a bit like trying to love ourselves. It won't happen. All that 'trying' does is create further feelings of worthlessness and hopelessness, and we abuse ourselves because we feel there is something wrong with us because we can't forgive.

Forgiveness is a process. It follows on from insight, anger, grief and acceptance. Acceptance means we have worked through the pain, anger and grief, and these feelings no longer hold us 'hostage' to the past. In the case of childhood abuse, we also come to realise that we are not a 'bad' or 'evil' person and that we are not the cause of the abuse. Acceptance for all of us, irrespective of our childhood backgrounds, means that we can move on with our life without bringing the past along with us in such painful ways.

Some people will move on to forgiveness; others will remain at the acceptance level. We need to do what is right for us. Either acceptance or forgiveness sets us free. But we need to work through the anger, pain and grief before we can do this. This is skilful compassionate action.

People will often say to me they are frightened that if they start crying they are never going to stop. This shows the depth and degree of the pain they are holding inside them. It shows clearly how much they have suppressed their emotions. These emotions need to be expressed, but be reassured they will stop crying once they have been released. Then they may then feel sadness for a while. Not depression, but sadness.

True sadness has poignancy to it. When this happened to me I couldn't work it out, because the sadness had a beauty and a gracefulness about it. I had never heard anyone speak about sadness in this way. Then, a couple of years later, I read about a specific meditation practice that talks about fear – the everyday fears that everyone has – and it also talks about anxiety. It says in part, 'Going beyond fear begins when we examine our fear, our anxiety . . . When we relax with our fear, we find sadness, which is calm and gentle . . . and perhaps romantic at the same time' (Trungpa, 1986). This is the beginning of true compassion, for ourselves and others.

Many people with an anxiety disorder say to me that this is exactly what they experience once they move beyond the fear. And in this sadness, the full strength and power of compassion arises.

If you are seeing a therapist, speak with them about any fears you may have about crying. Allow yourself to cry. You *will* stop!

Therapy is a partnership between ourselves and our therapists. And by working together, we can become free of the past and free to build our own future.

REAL SELF VERSUS ANXIETY SELF

As the recovery process gains momentum, we begin to have the experience of 'two selves' and many of us find this very confusing. Often we are too scared to talk about it because we are frightened we will be diagnosed with yet another disorder!

This experience of the two selves is part of the recovery process. We need to be mindful of how we can move between these two ways of being through our thoughts and perceptions.

The real self is the freedom and clarity we experience as a result of our growing emotional and intellectual integration. This state of being is very powerful, and we can feel the power it generates. We need to be aware of when we get caught up in our anxiety and panic thoughts again, as we will then move back into the 'anxiety disorder self'. We will feel disempowered and helpless.

People at this stage of recovery talk of the 'battle', the inner war they feel inside themselves. The anxiety disorder self throws every doubt, every fear, every symptom, every 'What if . . .?' it has at us. It is not going to give up easily. It has a vested interest in staying this way, because it 'protects' us from all we fear ourselves to be, or who we think we could become.

This is when we need to be skilful and take back responsibility for ourselves. When we do this, the feelings of freedom and clarity return and strengthen. This is the recovery process, and the more skilful we become, the more we begin to trust it and ourselves.

CASE HISTORY

Allen

Allen wanted to ask his friend a question. His friend was a psychologist. They had grown up together and there was a deep trust between them. But still Allen wondered what his friend was going to think of him when he asked his question. 'At least I now know where these fears come from,' he reassured himself. 'It's okay.'

Allen averted his eyes before speaking. 'I've suddenly realised that I am scared of myself,' Allen said to his friend. 'I am so scared that if I go any further with this recovery process, I am going to find that underneath all of this I am a bad person. A horrible person. That I am selfish and unkind. Or that I am going to turn into such a person. I don't like this very much,' he added with a wry smile as he looked at his friend again.

'Ah, Allen,' said his friend. 'This is the reason why people come so far in their recovery and then stop. This is the big one. This is the root fear. It means you have peeled away the final layer, Allen, and you have exposed the primary fear: "what if I am a bad, horrible person?" or "what if I become a bad horrible person?" This fear is the driving force of all of our thoughts, our beliefs and our need to be all things to all people.

'I can say all the usual things to you – that you won't be, that this won't happen – but it isn't going to help much. What I will say is that the one thing we don't realise is that the real self is not horrible, bad, selfish or unkind. But the only way you are going to know that is for you to allow the process to unfold further. There is simply no other way around it. It may not feel like it, Allen, but this is a major breakthrough.'

THE FINAL LAYER

The more we become aware, the more we peel away the layers. From the outer layers of our 'loud' panic and anxiety thoughts, through to the more subtle thoughts of 'What will people think?', until finally the root fear is exposed: 'What if I am or will become a bad person?' In the workshops and programs I run, this always becomes the number one issue. People are frightened of becoming themselves. They are scared they will find out that they are 'horrible', 'bad' people, and that they will be selfish and not caring towards others.

When we were children, hearing words like bad, horrible, selfish and unkind convinced us that we are all of these things. As children, we took these words to heart and we felt there was something fundamentally wrong with us. We still feel this. But the truth is there isn't anything wrong with us. We need to take the risk and find the truth of this for ourselves. There may be aspects of ourselves we may not like, but we don't have to act on them. If we understand them and how they developed, we can simply let them remain in our consciousness as a 'potential'.

This is why the demands of the self-esteem needs in Maslow's hierarchy of needs is so frightening. At the need to belong level we don't see the bigger picture, and we feel that taking care of ourselves and being responsible for ourselves means we are being selfish and uncaring. Bad, horrible people.

It comes back to choice. It is a matter of either staying where we are at this point, or allowing ourselves to feel this fear and continue the journey to get to know who we are. The more we practise skilful action, the more we realise that we are not a 'bad 'or 'horrible' person. We come to trust ourselves, and we become secure and safe within ourselves. In doing so, we trust other people with who we are.

As adults, we need to identify and understand all the factors that formed the fear we have of ourselves. And we need to become aware of all the reasons why our fear is *not* true. We need to ask ourselves the following questions:

- When I was a child, what was I told about myself?
- Were these 'throwaway' lines not meant to hurt, but to drive a point home?
- Were they said with intent?
- Can I see the driving force behind the person who said this to me?
- What 'messages' did I receive from my parents and others in relation to this?
- Can I understand why, as a child, I believed this about myself?
- Can I see why, as an adult, that I am not bad, selfish, horrible or unkind?

The practice of skilful action turns our beliefs about ourselves and other people upside down. We have been taught that compassion means giving selflessly. If not, it will mean we are bad, selfish, horrible or unkind. In some instances, people have been taught that their life must be one of selfless service to others, irrespective of their own needs. But we all need a healthy sense of self before we can 'give it away'!

SEPARATION ANXIETY

Most of us know the loneliness and emptiness we feel inside. We can be with people we love, we can be in the most intimate of situations, but the loneliness and emptiness remains with us. Many of us go out of our way to avoid these feelings by filling up our days and nights with a million and one things to do.

We may be alone during the day while other family members are out, and we spend the time talking with others on the phone or trying to fill our time in some form of communication with others. We find it difficult to sit and be with ourselves. When our anxiety disorder develops, our need to be with other people may increase tenfold.

The loneliness we feel is the degree of separation we have from ourselves. In needing to belong and in needing to be who we think we should be, we have abandoned and rejected ourselves. It is the ultimate separation anxiety.

So much of the emptiness and loneliness we feel inside is a direct result of our not accepting ourselves. We try to seek this acceptance through other people. Until we accept ourselves as we are right now, we will not be able to gain the confidence and skills necessary to develop a more whole and healthy, real sense of self. Our sense of self will continue to depend on other people's opinions of us and on our trying to prove there isn't something fundamentally wrong with us.

Instead of spending our lives trying to prove there isn't something 'wrong with us', we can learn to understand why there is nothing wrong with us at all. We can do this through skilful compassionate action.

We need to look at the reasons why we felt we needed to create a self that could fit in with who we perceived we needed to be. The child that we were did this in response to a very natural and normal need to belong, to be loved and cared for. Now, as adults, we need to accept all the reasons that have brought us to this point in our life. Not with disdain, but with compassion. And when we accept ourselves as we are, we then have a direction. This will enable us to change the aspects of ourselves that we feel are necessary for our emotional development and growth. This is taking responsibility for ourselves and it is treating ourselves with respect and dignity. Skilful compassion in action!

Part 5

Recovery

CHAPTER 16

The beginning

'I had been feeling fantastic,' said Sara. 'I felt that clarity and that freedom, but now I think I've hit some sort of wall. There was no anxiety, no panic, no depression, but also no sense of that freedom. It all feels so odd without the anxiety and the constant worry that it frightens me, so the anxiety is back. Any ideas?' she asked her counsellor.

'You're in no man's' land,' replied the counsellor, 'but at the moment you are looking at recovery from the "anxiety disorder" land. You simply don't see the bigger picture yet. You will,' said the counsellor reassuringly, 'as you continue to explore and get to know *you*.

'The first part of recovery is "peeling the onion", layer by layer. As we do, we peel away our outmoded beliefs and ways of being. And we reach "no man's land". This final stage of recovery is the rebuilding process. We have dismantled so much of our previous ways of being, and now we can rebuild on the much stronger foundations of our real self.

'In *The Wizard of Oz*, Dorothy always had the power to come home. She just didn't realise it. At this stage of recovery, we have already "doused the Wicked Witch of the West" and these final fears are just as dissolvable. Like Dorothy, you have the power to come home.'

The counsellor smiled gently at Sara. 'Follow your intuition. As your anxiety was your teacher, now in the rebuilding stage your intuition becomes your teacher. Listen to it and it will guide you wisely, as it teaches and shows you how to become all you could be.'

NO MAN'S LAND

As we begin to move into the final stage of recovery, it does feel 'odd'. It's not how we imagine recovery to be. During the recovery process we have periods of freedom and clarity and they are empowering and uplifting, and they show the promise and joy of full recovery. And we learn to sustain these periods by resolving the inner conflicts of who we think we should be. And one day we suddenly find ourselves in 'no man's land'. There is neither panic and anxiety nor freedom and clarity. We lose our identification of both ways of being. Suddenly we are a stranger to ourselves. We no longer have an anxiety disorder, and we no longer identify ourselves through the perceptions and expectations of ourselves and other people.

'No man's land' doesn't need to be frightening. When we understand it, it becomes exciting! In Chapter 14 I spoke of Maslow's hierarchy of needs, and of the process of our ongoing development. As we practise skilful action and take responsibility for ourselves, we begin to dis-identify with the 'need to belong level', and we begin to move to the next level of development, which is meeting our self-esteem needs.

To me, no man's land is the gap between these two levels. No man's land is a period of consolidation of the integration of the intellectual and emotional self. We are no longer divided by our internal conflicts of who we should be and of other people's perceptions and expectations of us. Paraphrasing Ken Wilber (Wilber, K, 1996), we have dis-identified with the need to belong level, but we have not yet stabilised at the self-esteem level. But we can. This is the final part of the full recovery process.

We peel way the various layers so that we can disengage all the various factors which generate our anxiety, panic and depression. And the final piece of the jigsaw puzzle falls into place when we recognise and let go of the root fear and dissolve this too with skilful action. As we do, we step off the rung of the need to belong level.

CASE HISTORIES

Deborah

It was one of those beautiful autumn evenings. The light from the setting sun filtered through the trees and their leaves blazed with colour. Deborah wondered how many other people were looking at this natural masterpiece as they hurried home after a day's work. Deborah knew that she had never taken much notice before. Now was different. Once or twice a day she would be struck by the beauty of her surroundings.

A moment here, a moment there. Those moments were precious in their spontaneity. They added to the peace she felt within herself.

Deborah was amazed at the last few years of her life. It had not always been like this. The years of panic disorder and agoraphobia had appeared to take everything from her. They were desolate years. The fight back was long and hard but she knew now that it had been worth it. Everything that had been taken away from her had been given back a thousand-fold. She was at peace with herself and she was free.

John

John was exhilarated. It was early morning and he had reached halfway in a 10-kilometre bike ride along the coast road. He wished he had brought his camera. John had loved photography ever since he was a child. He had always wanted to be a photographer, and now he was one.

John thought of his parents. They had worked hard to pay for his university fees, and they had been proud of him when he'd received his PhD and entered the world of academia. His ongoing anxiety had changed all that. As John had progressed towards recovery he'd realised that academic life was not for him. He'd struggled silently with the realisation for three years because he hadn't wanted to let his parents down. He'd even studied for another degree, hoping to combat his disquiet. It hadn't worked, and he'd made a break to follow his dreams of becoming a photographer. John knew he was taking a risk, but he knew it was worth it. He was free.

REBUILDING

Throughout the recovery process we have been developing the skills of compassion, self-responsibility and self-acceptance. As we do this, we are meeting our needs at the self-esteem level. As we step off the ladder at the 'need to belong' level, we already have the key components of the self-esteem level in place. Now we need to get to know who we are, so that we can fully identify with this next level of 'being'. As Ken Wilber (Wilber, 1996) writes, 'The interior world, for the first time, opens up before the mind's eye; psychological space becomes a new and exciting terrain'.

This stage of recovery is exciting, and the possibilities of who we can become are limitless. We are a 'blank canvas' and we get to choose what we paint and what colours we use! We can experiment and try all the things we have wanted to do throughout our life, but have felt frightened of doing because of what other people may think. Some of our ideas and desires we will let go, but others will take their place. Many of us are very creative people, and all the energy we have been using throughout our life to keep the real self suppressed is now free. We can use this energy to create a life we once only imagined.

INTUITION

We will become much more aware of our intuition, and if we listen to its gentle voice it will teach us and show us who we can become. How many times during our life have we ignored the quiet whisperings of self, which has always been trying to show us how we can be. Our anxiety disorder is more like a primal scream, shaking us to the very core in an effort for us to take notice. And when we reach no man's land, we again feel the gentle whisperings of the real self.

Philosopher Paul Brunton has commented, 'The intuitively governed mind is an undivided mind. It does not have to choose . . . or accept one or two alternatives. It does not suffer from being swayed this way and that by conflicting evidence, contradictory emotions or hesitant judgments.' (Brunton, 1988)

Skilful compassionate action resolves our inner conflicts, and our emotional development integrates with that of our intellectual development. Learning to listen and work with our intuition is the surest and safest way of learning to become all we can be. We feel the unity of the 'undivided' mind in the power and freedom of recovery, and we can live this freedom every day of our life.

We don't so much find happiness at the end of the rainbow. We are 'over the rainbow' and we find a life-sustaining joy in not being afraid of who we are.

AN EMAIL FROM ROSSI

Anxiety has been my main struggle, as you know, but I am holding on and working as well as I can at any particular point. Sometimes what makes me angry is that I've 'wasted' so much of my life having this anxiety disorder. And I can get totally absorbed in that anger.

Yet what is life really? It is a process, not a performance. And there is absolutely nothing we can do to turn it back and do some of it again. So that's where I scrounge around for a bit of humility for myself and say, okay, that has been my life these past few years, and it hasn't been all bad, and all of this is taking me somewhere. What am I learning from this process?

Wow, so many things that I might not otherwise have focused on, about myself and others. Acceptance, above all; gentleness and self-observation. And the deep, deep joy I sometimes experience when I am relaxed, in the moment, in connection with someone or nature. Would I have known that depth of joy without the struggle I have had?

Surely we don't achieve the deepest levels of love and joy without a struggle of some kind in our life.

APPENDIX

Early intervention/prevention

Have you just begun to experience panic attacks? Are you becoming extremely anxious for what appears to be no apparent reason? Has your doctor confirmed that you are experiencing panic attacks, anxiety, or both?

It is important that you do not self-diagnose. Diagnosis needs to be done by your doctor. Panic attacks and anxiety can mimic a number of physical conditions, so you need your doctor to assess and confirm that your symptoms are those of panic and anxiety. Once you have been diagnosed, you are then in a position to be able to minimise or prevent any potential development of an anxiety disorder.

Like all of us who have experienced panic attacks and anxiety, you would be feeling quite frightened and confused. You would have heard people talk of having panic attacks, either in the media, or a family member or a friend may have told you of their experience. However, hearing about them is one thing, actually having a panic attack or experiencing extreme anxiety, or both, is another! The words 'panic attack' and 'anxiety' don't convey the ferocity of the experience. So when it happens to you, there doesn't seem to be any correlation between your understanding of the meaning of these words and your actual experience.

You will be wondering what is happening to you and why it is happening. You will be trying to 'pull yourself together'. You may be trying to 'think positive', but your efforts are only partially effective or perhaps not effective at all. You may have begun to search the internet for information to help you understand your experience. You may have been reading bulletin boards or participated in chat rooms to speak with people with similar experiences. While this may have provided some degree of reassurance, you could also be feeling even more frightened by what you have learned.

You will have found that some people can have an anxiety disorder for years and that many people also struggle with the secondary effects of their disorder, including agoraphobia, depression, perhaps a prescribed drug addiction or alcohol dependency. You may have even been told by your doctor that you will just have to learn to live with it, or that you will be on medication for the rest of your life.

What you may not have learnt is that people no longer need to 'learn to live with it'. In the past, there were very few effective treatment options available. Now there are. Anxiety disorders have only been recognised since 1980, and it has only been since the mid-1990s that many more people are being correctly diagnosed within a reasonable time frame. However, early diagnosis does not necessarily mean that people are being offered effective treatment strategies, such as cognitive behavioural therapy.

It is the lack of an immediate diagnosis and/or lack of effective treatment strategies that leads to the development of an anxiety disorder and the secondary conditions associated to them. This can also be why many people are told by their doctors that they will need to 'learn to live with it', as their doctors have not seen people recover in the long term.

Much of the suffering that appears to be inherent in anxiety disorders is actually preventable. The majority of people who have had panic disorder will say that if they had been diagnosed in the beginning, had understood from the beginning, had known how to manage their panic attacks from the beginning, they would not have gone onto develop their anxiety disorder. It is an ongoing tragedy that early intervention strategies are rarely used to minimise or prevent the development of an anxiety disorder. Many of the treatment options available can be more reactive than proactive, and they inadvertently contribute to the development and perpetuation of anxiety disorders.

While so many people commit to caring for their physical health, most of us do not commit to caring for our mental health. Working with early intervention strategies means making this commitment to ourselves. Our mental health is just as important as our physical health, and early intervention strategies can assist us in protecting it. Although there are no specific resources available for early intervention, there is still much you can do to prevent or minimise any possible development of a disorder.

Understanding

The first question everyone asks is, 'What is happening to me?' As I noted above, the words 'panic attacks' and 'anxiety' do not describe the actual feeling state of these experiences. The feeling state is much more than these three words can convey. This is why it is so important for us to learn and understand the dynamics of our experience. The more we understand, the less fear we have, which makes our panic attacks and anxiety easier to control. Knowledge and understanding of our experience is power.

In many instances, our doctor doesn't give us an adequate explanation of our experience. We may be told we are having panic attacks or anxiety and just be given a prescription for medication. This leaves many people feeling confused and frightened. Often people feel too awkward or embarrassed to ask their doctor for a more detailed explanation. This is a big mistake! There is no reason to feel awkward or embarrassed. Our doctors see many people with panic attacks and anxiety so it is important we don't let these feelings prevent us from asking for more detailed information. We don't realise that some doctors assume we understand what is happening to us, and may be surprised that we don't.

While we may be given a prescription for medication, it is also important that we ask our doctor about early intervention strategies such as cognitive therapy. Mindfulness or other cognitive therapies can assist us in learning to work with and control the thoughts that create so much of our distress and confusion. If our doctor doesn't offer or isn't able to provide such strategies, we need to ask them to refer us to a mindfulness or other cognitive behavioural therapist, who will be able to assist us in these strategies.

The more knowledge and understanding we have about our attacks and anxiety, the easier it is to accept and work with our experience. Anxiety disorder organisations, either local or via the internet, can provide additional information and referral to cognitive behavioural therapists, and may also be able to provide telephone support, access to support groups and other resources.

The second question everyone asks is, 'Why is this happening to me?' I discuss the answer to this under 'Causes' in Chapter 3.

INITIAL FEARS

One of the major reasons why people go on to develop an anxiety disorder is because they are frightened that their doctor has made a mistake in the diagnosis. They can also fear that their clinical test results have been mixed up with someone else's. This fear is a direct consequence of the 'feeling' experience of a panic attack and/or anxiety and the actual words used to describe it: 'panic attack', 'anxiety'.

It is important to discuss this fear with our doctor. We may feel embarrassed or perhaps frightened, but we need to. The fear that our doctor may have made a mistake only fuels our fear, which makes us more vulnerable to further panic attacks and anxiety.

Some people will get a second opinion and this can be extremely helpful if it assists us in accepting the diagnosis. It is when we seek a third or fourth or perhaps tenth opinion that we need to stop, and begin the process of believing and accepting the diagnosis. If we don't accept it, our fear can be the major driver of the development of an anxiety disorder.

We all need to understand and accept the sensations and symptoms of our panic attacks and our anxiety for what they are. Panic and anxiety. Nothing more. They can make us feel as if are going to die, have a heart attack, go insane, lose control or embarrass ourselves in some way – 'can make us feel' being the operative words. We do not die, go insane or lose control through panic and anxiety. This is what a panic attack feels like. This is what high anxiety feels like. We need to believe it and accept it.

Many of us get caught up in the thoughts, 'This is not me, I am not like this . . .' 'I am the strong one in the family . . .' 'I am extroverted, the life of the party . . .' 'How can this be happening to me?' Most of us think this! Being strong, which we are, being extroverted, which some of us can be, does not exempt us from panic and anxiety. Anxiety disorders are equal opportunity disorders. They do not discriminate!

Our confusion and fears can be compounded if we tell other people. We get caught up in their exclamations, 'Don't be silly, you are not like that! You are too strong.' This only adds to our confusion and fear because we think society's perception, and perhaps ours, is that people with anxiety are 'weak' and should just 'pull themselves together'.

The fear and stigma of mental disorders and illness within the community is also a factor. We begin to feel extremely ashamed, especially if our panic or anxiety increases no matter how hard we try and 'pull ourselves together'. What we don't realise is that the shame we feel about ourselves increases our fear, which increases our anxiety, which continues fuelling our fear and around and around we go. Having panic attacks, anxiety, an anxiety disorder or a mental illness is nothing to be ashamed about. We have heard this before in one form or another, and while we may agree with this in relation to other people, the time has now come for us to begin to believe the truth of this in relation to ourselves.

The fact is we don't have anything to be ashamed about. Millions of people worldwide experience panic attacks and anxiety. The more we resist accepting our experience, the more we increase the potential for developing an anxiety disorder. Knowledge, understanding and acceptance of our experience diminish this potential.

CASE HISTORIES

Anthony

Anthony walked out of the doctor's office. He didn't know what to think. This was the third doctor he had seen about his symptoms. Like the other two doctors, he confirmed to Anthony that he was experiencing panic attacks.

A few days before, Anthony had been woken during the night with what he thought was a heart attack. His wife had called the ambulance, and he had been taken to the hospital where they ran a series of tests. The results showed that there was nothing physically wrong with him. The doctor at the hospital told him his symptoms were those of a panic attack. Anthony knew that he had been feeling quite stressed at work, and had not been sleeping well as a result and been skipping meals. That happened for lots of people and they didn't have a panic attack, they just got on with it all. 'And so should I,' he thought to himself. But he was filled with doubt.

Anthony went to his office and tried to work. He could not stop thinking that the doctors had made a mistake, and that the test results at the hospital had been mixed up. He searched the internet and read a number of websites that dealt with panic attacks. Although the symptoms seemed to be the same, he couldn't help but think his symptoms were different, that they meant there was something physically wrong with him. 'I have to do something,' he thought to himself.

One doctor had prescribed medication; the doctor at the hospital had concurred. The other doctor had referred him to a cognitive behavioural therapist. He told Anthony to 'draw a line in the sand' and begin to accept that his experience was that of panic and anxiety. He also told Anthony that he needed to be taught how to manage his attacks so he could prevent his panic and anxiety from increasing. 'Why not?' Anthony thought to himself. 'Perhaps the therapist could help him.' He rang and made an appointment.

Camille

Camille was running late for work. She hurried out of her apartment, locked the door and ran to catch the bus before it pulled away from the stop. She made it with moments to spare. She relaxed back in her seat, thankful that she wasn't going to be late for work. Camille didn't like rushing around in the morning; she was always concerned that she would forget something. Then the thought came, 'Did I turn the heater off in the bedroom?' 'Of course I did,' she thought. She went back over what she had done before leaving for work. She could not remember turning off the heater. Camille became increasingly agitated. If the heater was on, it could cause a major problem. Her towel had been draped over it. There was no one to ask to check it for her, as her husband was away on business and he had the only other key. 'I am going to have to go home to check,' Camille thought, 'but how can I? I will be late for work.' Her thoughts raced back and forth. Will she or won't she go back home?

Camille moved out of her seat and made her way to the door of the bus. There really wasn't a choice. She needed to go home to check. She crossed the road and walked to the bus stop to catch a bus home. Once she was home, she walked into the bedroom. The heater was on and the towel was feeling very hot. She turned off the heater, hung up the towel in the bathroom and went to work.

Two days later, it happened again. This time, Camille found that she had indeed turned the heater off and removed the towel before she'd left for work. A week later it happened again. And again. And yet again.

Camille was feeling desperate. She could not keep on being late for work. She had already been warned that she could lose her job. Although she felt extremely anxious she did not want to bother her doctor, because she wasn't sick and he would think she was going mad. She resigned instead.

Michelle

'Oh no, not again, please no,' Michelle pleaded to herself. 'I can't believe it, how can I have another panic attack? I thought it was all over.'

Michelle had panic disorder/agoraphobia ten years ago. With a combination of medication and seeing a counsellor she overcame it and she thought herself to be recovered. Now it was back, and back with a vengeance. It seemed as though it was trying to make up for those ten years when she didn't have a panic attack. 'What if I go back to agoraphobia? What if I can't go to work? Can't drive?'

Michelle did a search on panic disorder on the internet and was surprised at the number of websites and treatment options now available. Among the sites were a couple that talked about prevention and how she could prevent a relapse. 'Whatever it takes,' she thought to herself as she reached for the phone to make an appointment with her doctor to discuss her options.

There is much we can do to help ourselves prevent or minimise any potential for the development of an anxiety disorder. I have highlighted these below in the form of a 'check list'. The topics are discussed throughout the book.

You will have times when you will feel overwhelmed with feelings of confusion and fear. This is part of the overall experience of panic and anxiety. When you are feeling this way, come back to the check list and see what you need to work on so that you can break through these feelings. The more knowledge you have, the more you will understand your experience, the more you can minimise or prevent any possible transition to an anxiety disorder.

THE BASICS

- Once you have been diagnosed as having panic attacks, anxiety or an anxiety disorder, you need to make a commitment to yourself and your mental health to gain a detailed understanding of what you are experiencing.
- Build your knowledge of panic attacks and anxiety by asking your doctor to explain to you in detail exactly what is happening to you. Ask your doctor to clarify any points you do not understand. Remember: your doctor may not realise that you do not understand how your experience fits into the words 'panic attacks' and 'anxiety'.
- Read as much as you can about panic attacks and anxiety disorders. Talk with your local anxiety disorder association, as they can provide you with information and referrals to anxiety disorder specialists.
- The internet is a valuable resource of information with thousands of websites dedicated to anxiety disorders. Be mindful though, as some anxiety disorder chat rooms and

bulletin boards can give the impression that people need to 'learn to live with their disorder'. Many people are still not aware that recovery is possible.

- Recognise that most people have not had access to early intervention strategies and many people have never had access to effective long-term treatment options. Some people may also have underlying personal issues, which they are not discussing publicly, and these issues can be a factor in maintaining their anxiety disorder.
- Don't take their experiences and their difficulties as indications that 'this will happen to you'. Early intervention strategies can help to prevent this.

EARLY INTERVENTION STRATEGIES

We all need to recognise and accept:

- The words 'panic attack' and 'anxiety' do not sufficiently describe the overall, actual feeling state of our experience.
- This is what a panic attack feels like. This is what extreme anxiety feels like.
- They are not what we think they are.
- People do not die, go insane or lose control through panic attacks and anxiety.
- You will not be the first one this happens to.
- The 'big one' does not happen!
- There is a 'genetic contribution to the development of panic disorder' (APA, 1994).
- Panic attacks and/or anxiety develop for any number of reasons, including a current or recent past major life stress, a build-up of stress, physical illness, influenza or another virus, marijuana or other similar drugs.

- It is not your fault that this has happened to you.
- Panic attacks and anxiety do not discriminate. They are equal opportunity disorders.
- They are not a sign of an inherent weakness within you.
- Having panic attacks or an anxiety disorder is nothing to be embarrassed or ashamed about.
- You are not alone in this experience. Fourteen per cent of the Australian population (ABS, 2009) also experience panic attacks and anxiety, and other people feel exactly as you do.
- This is a confusing and difficult time.
- Take time out every day to meditate or to practise another relaxation technique.
- Refuse to become caught up in the 'what ifs' and its variants.
- Take control of your thoughts by learning mindfulness or other cognitive skills.
- Make informed decisions about treatment options.
- Ask your doctor about early intervention strategies and a referral to a therapist who is experienced in mindfulness or another cognitive technique.
- Recognise that medication is not necessarily an early intervention strategy in preventing the development of an anxiety disorder.
- Become informed about any medication you decide to take: what type is it, how does it work, are there any possible side effects or any possible withdrawal or discontinuation effects?
- Recognise that if you do need medication, don't perceive this as a 'weakness' or failure. It isn't.

SELF-ESTEEM

- Recognise that low self-esteem undermines the way we deal with stress, whether day-to-day or major life stress, and undermines how we manage our panic attacks and anxiety.
- Thinking we are weak, a failure, pathetic, hopeless or helpless is detrimental to our mental health and fuels our attacks and anxiety.
- Being responsible for everyone else, trying to make people happy, solving their problems and always saying yes is betraying our responsibility to ourselves and will create additional anxiety and panic.
- Trying to be all things to all people is detrimental to our mental health.
- The need to be perfect in all we do ensures we do not have a 'perfect' quality of life.

EARLY INTERVENTION CHECK LIST

Do you:

☐ Believe and accept that you do have panic attacks or anxiety?

☐ Believe and accept that this is what the experience of panic attacks and anxiety feels like?

☐ Understand and accept why your fears associated with your panic attacks and anxiety will not happen?

Are you:

☐ Thinking, 'This is not me, I am not like this'? Can you see how this creates further anxiety?

☐ Confident that your doctor has not made a mistake in the diagnosis or do you feel as though they have missed something?

☐ Confident that you have told your doctor everything that is happening to you?

☐ Trying to be the 'perfect' patient?

☐ Learning and understanding all you need to know about panic attacks and anxiety?

☐ Taking time out each day to meditate or use another form of relaxation?

☐ Learning to see the causes of each of your individual panic attacks?

☐ Learning to see the causes of your anxiety?

☐ Understanding the principles involved in mindfulness or other cognitive strategies?

☐ Working with these?

☐ Possibly having side effects from your medication? Have you spoken to your doctor about this?

☐ Taking the prescribed amount of medication at the pre-scribed time?

☐ Is your commitment to yourself and your mental health your number one priority?

Reviewing your answers, can you see the points you need to work on?

Glossary

CBT	cognitive behaviour therapy
GAD	generalised anxiety disorder
OCD	obsessive compulsive disorder
PD	panic disorder
PTSD	post-traumatic stress disorder
SA	social anxiety

Further information

For further information, visit Bronwyn's website:
panicattacks.com.au

Telephone counselling is available with Bronwyn. For an appointment, contact:
Australian residents: (08) 8411 1106
International residents: 61 8 8411 1106

Bronwyn's Panic Anxiety Management Workshop DVDs and a double CD featuring a meditation designed for people with an anxiety disorder are available from Bronwyn's website.

Bibliography

American Psychiatric Association, 1994, *Diagnostic and Statistical Manual of Mental Disorders*, 4th edition, APA, Washington.

Argyle, N. & Roth, M., 1990, 'The phenomenological study of 90 patients with panic disorder', *Psychiatric Developments*, vol. 7, no. 3, pp. 187–209, cited in Argyle, N. et al., 1991, 'The structure of phobias in panic disorder', *British Journal of Psychiatry*, vol. 59, pp. 378–82.

Arthur-Jones, J. & Fox, B., 1994, *Cross Cultural Comparisons of Panic Disorder*, Panic Anxiety Hub, Goolwa.

Arthur-Jones, J. & Fox, B., 1997, *Treatment Needs of People with an Anxiety Disorder*, Panic Anxiety Disorder Association Inc., Adelaide.

Australian Bureau of Statistics, March 2009, ABS Catalogue No. 4102.0 – Australian Social Trends.

Benson, H., 1975, *The Relaxation Response*, William Morrow, New York.

Boyd, J. H. & Crump, T., 1991, 'Westphal's Agoraphobia', *Journal of Anxiety Disorders*, vol. 5, pp. 77–86.

Branden, N., 1994, *The Six Pillars of Self-Esteem*, Bantam Books, New York.

Brayley, J., Bradshaw, G. & Pols, R., 1991, *Guidelines for the*

Prevention and Management of Benzodiazepine Dependence, AGPS, Canberra.

British Medical Journal, 1998, 'Editorial: Antidepressant discontinuation reactions', vol. 316, pp. 1105–06.

Brown, G. W. & Harris, T. O., 1993, 'Aetiology of anxiety and depressive disorders in an inner-city population', 1. 'Early adversity', *Psychological Medicine*, vol. 23, pp. 143–54.

Brunton, P., 1988, *The Notebooks of Paul Brunton*, vol. 14 *Inspiration and the Overself*, Paul Brunton Philosophic Foundation, Larson Publications, New York.

Commission of Public Affairs & the Division of Public Affairs of the American Psychiatrists Association, 1990, *Information Booklet on Anxiety Disorders*, APA, Washington.

Fewtrell, W. D. & O'Connor, K. P., 1988, 'Dizziness and depersonalisation', *Adv. Behav. Res. Ther.*, vol. 10, pp. 201–18.

Hafner, J., 1986, *Marriage and Mental Illness*, Guilford Press, New York.

Kabat-Zinn, J., Massion, A., Kristeller, J., Peterson, L. G., Fletcher, K. E., Pbert, L., Lendeking, L. & Santorelli, S. F., 1992, 'Effectiveness of a meditation-based stress-reduction program in the treatment of anxiety disorders', *American Journal of Psychiatry*, vol. 149, no. 7, pp. 936–43.

Kenardy, J., Oei, T. P. S., Ryan, P. & Evans, L., 1988, 'Attribution of panic attacks: Patient perspective', *Journal of Anxiety Disorders*, vol. 2, pp. 243–51.

Knott, V. J., 1990, 'Neuroelectrical activity related to panic disorder', *Progress in Neuro-Psychpharmacology and Biological Psychiatry*, vol. 14, pp. 697–707.

Maslow, A., 1954, *Motivation and Personality*, Harper & Row, New York, cited in Wilbur K, 1990, *Eye to Eye: The Quest for the New Paradigm*, Shambhala Publications, Inc, Boston.

Index

Acceptance 105, 111–13, 228,
    234–5
  non-acceptance 107, 112, 200
Agoraphobia – avoidance 38–9,
    40–2, 106
  anticipatory anxiety 41–2, 208
  feeling unwell 42
  graded exposure 75–6,
    204–208
  housebound 38
  overall defence 40
  protection 106
Alcohol 45, 84, 189, 209
Anger 69, 103, 116, 184
  check list 185
Anti-depressants 62, 81, 84–5
  check list 84
  discontinuation reactions 78,
    79, 81
Anxiety 25, 50, 125, 154–5, 158,
    171, 172, 200
  as our teacher 222, 228
  growth 229
  separation 239–40
Anxiety disorders 24, 253, 257
  acceptance of 114
    first stage 115
    revisited 199–200

second stage 116
  stages of 115
    third stage 116
behaviour theory 28
biological model 27
combinations 34
generalised anxiety disorder
    33
obsessive compulsive disorder
    31–32
panic disorder 29–30
post traumatic stress disorder
    32–33
psychodynamic theory 27
secondary conditions 37,
    253
social phobia 30–1, 38
understanding 25, 96

Benson, Herbert 134
Bibliography 268
Boundaries 224
Brunton, Paul 250

Chemical imbalance 27
Childhood abuse 33, 57, 60, 87,
    235
Cognitive techniques 73

Cognitive behavioural therapy
74, 77, 79, 80, 89
Compassion 105, 108, 225, 235

Depersonalisation 20, 28, 51,
56, 57
Depression 37, 43, 125
Derealisation 20, 28, 51, 56
Diagnosis 50, 200, 252, 256
Dissociative symptoms 65

Early intervention/prevention 26,
252
anxiety disorders 37
the basics 261
cognitive therapy 255
early intervention strategies
254, 262, 264
initial fears 256–7
self esteem 264
understanding 254
Eating difficulties 63, 209
Emotions 103, 230
Expectations 226

Family 43, 203
Fatigue 63
Fear
hoarding in case needed 32
major fear 30, 183
of being judged 30
of blushing 30
of contamination by germs 32
of dying 30
of embarrassment 30
of going insane 30
of having a heart attack 30
of having a stroke 30
of leaving appliances on 32

of losing control in some way
30
of making a fool of one's self
30
of suffering from a brain
tumour 30
root 238, 247
Flashbacks 32
Forgiveness 234

Generalised anxiety disorder *see
Anxiety disorders*
Goals 211
Graded exposure *see Agoraphobia*
Growth anxiety 229
Guilt 160, 222–4

Hypnotherapy 88
Hypochondria 64, 200

Intuition 249

Loneliness 239–41
Loss
of feelings 62
of libido 62

Maslow, Abraham 215
hierarchy of needs 215–17,
222, 225, 246–7
self-esteem needs 238
Medication 77–9, 208
anti-depressants 81
check list 82–5
discontinuation reactions 78
interactions with other
medications 78
side effects 78
tranquillisers 80

Medication (*Cont.*)
  withdrawal 80
Meditation 125
  as a release 131
  awareness 142
  becoming relaxed 137
  breathing technique 134
  do not disturb 130
  effects of 149
  image technique 135
  mindfulness 126, 128, 135
  need to be in control 147–9
  observing thoughts 132–3
  practice of 135–6
  questions and answers
    141–52
  when and where 129
  why 126
  word technique 134
Mental health plan 77
Mindfulness as a cognitive
    technique 73–4, 104, 164,
    166–9, 208, 213, 231
  check list one 171
  check list two 174–5
  check list three 178
  dissociation 170
  letting go of thoughts 175
  letting it happen 178–81
  summary 183

Need to belong 217–21
Need to be in control 48–9
Need to be perfect 70, 211
Nightmares 32
No man's land 246–7

Obsessive compulsive disorder
  see Anxiety disorders

Panic attacks 15–16, 19–21
  early intervention/prevention
    252–65
  nocturnal 28, 58, 62
  situationally predisposed 21
  specific 21
  spontaneous 20–1
Panic disorder *see Anxiety
  disorders*
Passivity 99, 103
Perception 97, 153–5, 216
  change of 107, 165–7, 178,
    197
Positive thinking 161
Post traumatic stress disorder *see
  Anxiety disorders*
Prevention 28, 252–64
Psychotherapy 87–8, 230–6

Recovery 28, 64, 74, 90
  first layer 193
  issues 189
  layers of 115–17
  number one priority 192–3
  rebuilding 249
  relearning 210
  second layer 201
  setbacks 196
  third layer 215
  with attitude 184
  working through process
    194–6
Responsibility to self 117, 119

Sadness 87, 103, 230, 235
Self absorption 47–8, 58
Self created 100–1
Self esteem 97, 217–22, 238,
    247, 249, 264

sense of self 95–6, 99, 214
Self real 101, 104, 194, 236,
    249
Self responsibility 103, 105, 107,
    117, 119–20, 214, 249
Setbacks 194, 196–9
    check list 210
Skilful compassionate action
    105
Sleeping difficulties 62
'So what' 155–6
Social phobia *see Anxiety disorders*
Statistics 24
Stress 26–7, 57, 106, 201–3
    threshold to 190, 194–9

Symptoms 50
    check list 65

Taking care of ourselves 209, 238
Therapies 69
    other 88
    overview 89
Tranquilisers 80
    check list 83
    withdrawal 80, 208
Trust in self 232, 233, 238

What if 42, 47, 53, 76, 156, 158,
    228
Wilber, K 215–16, 247, 249